Incitement to Terrorism

Nijhoff Law Specials

VOLUME 95

The titles published in this series are listed at *brill.com/nlsp*

Incitement to Terrorism

Edited by

Anne F. Bayefsky
Laurie R. Blank

BRILL
NIJHOFF

LEIDEN | BOSTON

Library of Congress Cataloging-in-Publication Data

Names: Bayefsky, Anne F., editor. | Blank, Laurie R., editor.
Title: Incitement to terrorism / Edited by Anne Bayefsky, Laurie Blank.
Description: Leiden : Brill Nijhoff, 2018. | Series: Nijhoff law specials ; VOLUME 95 | Includes bibliographical references and index.
Identifiers: LCCN 2017061438 (print) | LCCN 2018000745 (ebook) | ISBN 9789004359826 (E-book) | ISBN 9789004359819 (pbk. : alk. paper)
Subjects: LCSH: Hate speech--Law and legislation. | Hate crimes--Law and legislation. | Terrorism. | Freedom of speech.
Classification: LCC KZ7177.I53 (ebook) | LCC KZ7177.I53 I53 2018 (print) | DDC 345/.02317--dc23
LC record available at https://lccn.loc.gov/2017061438

Typeface for the Latin, Greek, and Cyrillic scripts: "Brill". See and download: brill.com/brill-typeface.

ISSN 0924-4549
ISBN 978-90-04-35981-9 (paperback)
ISBN 978-90-04-35982-6 (e-book)

This book is printed on acid-free paper and produced in a sustainable manner.

Contents

List of Contributors

Micah Avni

is a lawyer and CEO of Peninsula Group Ltd., a publically-traded Israeli commercial finance institution. He was ranked among the 100 most influential people in Israel by The Marker Magazine in both 2015 and 2016. After his father, Richard Lakin, was brutally murdered by terrorists in October 2015, Micah founded Stop Incitement, a movement whose mission is to rid social media of incitement to hatred, violence and terror. Mr. Avni holds a Law degree from the Hebrew University and a joint MBA degree from the Kellogg School of Management at Northwestern University and the Recanati Graduate School of Business Administration at Tel Aviv University. Prior to his legal studies, he served as a Commander in one of the Israel Defense Force's elite combat units.

Anne F. Bayefsky

is a Professor and Director of the Touro Institute on Human Rights and the Holocaust (a UN-accredited NGO), as well as the President of Human Rights Voices. She is a member of the International Law Association's Committee on Human Rights in Times of Emergency. Professor Bayefsky has taught at York University, the University of Ottawa Law Faculty, and Columbia University Law School. She has served on both governmental and non-governmental organizations to the United Nations for over thirty years. She served with the Canadian delegation to the UN General Assembly and the Commission on Human Rights, and with non-governmental delegations to UN world conferences in Vienna, Beijing and Durban, as well as to the Human Rights Council. She has been a member of the External Research Advisory Committee of the UN High Commissioner for Refugees, and a member of the Advisory Panel of UNDP on the UN Development Report. She is the author or editor of 11 books in the areas of international and constitutional human rights law, and the recipient of Canada's highest human rights research award, the Bora Laskin National Fellowship in Human Rights Research.

Laurie R. Blank

is Clinical Professor of Law and Director of the International Humanitarian Law Clinic at Emory University School of Law. She is the co-author of International Law and Armed Conflict: Fundamental Principles and Contemporary Challenges in the Law of War, a casebook on the law of war (with G. Noone, Aspen Publishing 2013). She is also the co-director of a multi-year project on military training programs in the law of war and the co-author of Law of War Training: Resources for Military and Civilian Leaders (USIP 2008, with G. Noone, second edition 2013). In addition, she is the series editor of the ICRC's teaching supplements on IHL, and was a member of the American Bar Association's Advisory Committee to the Standing Committee on Law and National Security and the Public Interest Law and Policy Group's High Level Working Group on Piracy. Before coming to Emory, she was a program officer in the Rule of Law Program at the United States Institute of Peace. At USIP, she directed the Experts' Working Group on International Humanitarian Law, in particular a multi-year project focusing on New Actors in the Implementation and Enforcement of International Humanitarian Law.

Geoffrey S. Corn

is the Vinsen & Elkins Professor of Law at South Texas College of Law in Houston Texas. Prior to joining the South Texas faculty in 2005, he served in the U.S. Army for 21 years (1983–2004), as an officer, and a final year as a civilian legal advisor, retiring in the rank of Lieutenant Colonel. His teaching and scholarship focuses on the law of armed conflict, national security law, criminal law and procedure, and prosecutorial ethics. He has appeared as an expert witness at the Military Commission in Guantanamo, the International Criminal Tribunal for the Former Yugoslavia, and in federal court. He is the lead author of *The Law of Armed Conflict: An Operational Perspective* (Aspen), and *The Laws of War and the War on Terror* (Oxford University Press), and *National Security Law and Policy: a Student Treatise* (Aspen), and *Military Operations: U.S. Law, Policy, and Practice* (OUP). His Army career included service as the Army's senior law of war expert advisor, tactical intelligence officer in Panama; supervisory defense counsel for the Western United States; Chief of International Law for US Army Europe; Professor of International and National Security Law at the US Army Judge Advocate General's School; Chief Prosecutor for the 101st Airborne Division.

Robert R. Friedmann

is founding director of the Georgia International Law Enforcement Exchange and Professor Emeritus of Criminal Justice at Georgia State University's Andrew Young School of Policy Studies. He was the Distinguished Chair of Public Safety Partnerships (2007–2010) and served as Chair (1989–2002) of the Criminal Justice Department at Georgia State University. His interest and published work focus on community policing, terrorism, and crime analysis. His books include: *Community Policing: Comparative Perspectives and Prospects*, (1992), *Criminal Justice in Israel: An Annotated Bibliography of English Language Publications, 1948–1993* (1995), *Crime and Criminal Justice in Israel:*

Assessing the Knowledge Base toward the Twenty-First Century (1998), *A Diary of Four Years of Terrorism and Anti-Semitism: 2000–2004* (2005; two volumes), and *28 Letters* (2012). He serves on the advisory board of the International Institute for Counter-Terrorism, Herzliya, Israel, the Research Institute for European and American Studies, Athens, Greece, and is a member of the executive committee of The International Counter-Terrorism Academic Community. He works closely with a number of police departments, in the U.S. and internationally, on community policing and homeland security.

Gregory S. Gordon
is Associate Professor at the Chinese University of Hong Kong Faculty of Law, where he previously served as Associate Dean (Development/External Affairs) and Director of the Research Postgraduates Programme. Prior to joining CUHK, he was a law professor at the University of North Dakota and served as Director of its Center for Human Rights and Genocide Studies. Professor Gordon served as an attorney with the Office of the Prosecutor of the International Criminal Tribunal for Rwanda on the landmark "Media Cases," the first international post-Nuremberg incitement prosecutions of media executives. For this work, he received a commendation from the U.S. Attorney General. He subsequently worked with the U.S. Department of Justice, serving, in sequence, as a street crime, white collar, organized crime and then human rights prosecutor. While at DOJ, he was detailed to Sierra Leone to conduct a post-civil war justice assessment. He has been featured on CNN, C-SPAN, NPR, the BBC and Radio France Internationale and was the BBC World News live television analyst for the announcement of the historic Charles Taylor trial verdict. His book *Atrocity Speech Law: Foundation, Fragmentation, Fruition* (OUP, 2017), proposes a new paradigm for treating hate speech in international criminal law. In 2018, he was selected as a Research Fellow of the Centre for International Law Research and Policy.

Amos N. Guiora
is Professor at the S.J. Quinney College of Law, University of Utah. He teaches Criminal Procedure, International Law, Global Perspectives on Counterterrorism and Religion and Terrorism. Professor Guiora was a Member of the American Bar Association's Law and National Security Advisory Committee from 2010–2014, and is currently a Research Associate at the University of Oxford, Oxford Institute for Ethics, Law and Armed Conflict. He is also a Research Fellow at the International Institute on Counter-Terrorism, The Interdisciplinary Center, Herzylia, Israel. In addition, he is a Corresponding Member, The Netherlands School of Human Rights Research, the University of Utrecht School of Law. Professor Guiora is the author of several books and book chapters, most

recently: The Crime of Complicity: The Bystander in the Holocaust (2017), which has helped build a foundation for duty to assist legislation in the state of Utah; In the Crosshairs of Unfettered Executive Power: The Moral Dilemmas of Justifying and Carrying Out Targeted Killings (2015); Targeted killings: Defining and Applying the Limits of Military Ethics (2015); Establishing a Drone Court: Restraints on the Executive Branch; First Amendment and National Security (2015); and Global Perspectives on Cybersecurity (2016). He served for 19 years in the Israel Defense Forces as Lieutenant Colonel (retired), and held a number of senior command positions, including Commander of the IDF School of Military Law and Legal Advisor to the Gaza Strip.

Asa Kasher

is the Laura Schwarz-Kipp Professor Emeritus of Professional Ethics and Philosophy of Practice, and Professor Emeritus of Philosophy, Tel Aviv University. In 2000 he received the Israel Prize, the country's highest national prize, for his contribution to philosophy. His research covers a broad range of topics in philosophy and ethics, especially including military ethics, medical ethics and the philosophy of language as well as issues of Jewish identity. He is a member of the European Academy of Science and Humanities and has taught at Tel Aviv University, Bar-Ilan University, The University of Texas at Austin, UCLA, IDF College of Command, the Center of Military and Strategic Studies and the University of Calgary. Holding an M.SC. in Mathematics, Applied Mathematics and History and Philosophy of Science and a PhD. in Philosophy from the Hebrew University of Jerusalem, he is the author of The Israel Defense Force's Code of Ethics first published by the Israel Ministry of Defense in 1994 and has worked with others on the Code of Ethics of the Knesset and the Code of Ethics of the Ministers. He has recently been engaged in developing the code of ethics of the Ministry of Defence and a new code of ethics for Israeli Police, among other agencies and organizations.

Christian Leuprecht

is Class of 1965 Professor in Leadership at the Royal Military College of Canada, Matthew Flinders Fellow at Flinders University in South Australia, Munk Senior Fellow at the Macdonald Laurier Institute, and cross-appointed to Queen's University. He is an elected member of the College of New Scholars of the Royal Society of Canada. He also holds a Governor-in-Council appointment to the Executive Committee of the governing Council of NSERC, and is president of the International Sociological Association's Research Committee on Armed Forces and Conflict Resolution. An expert on security and defense, political demography, and comparative federalism and multilevel governance, he is regularly called as an expert witness to testify before committees of the Canadian Parliament. His publications have appeared in English, German, French, and Spanish and include nine books and scores of articles that have appeared, for instance, in *Electoral Studies*, *Armed Forces and Society*, *Global Crime*, the *Canadian Foreign Policy Journal*, the *Canadian Journal of Political Science*, and *Terrorism and Political Violence*.

David Matas
is a lawyer in private practice. He specializes in refugee, immigration and human rights law in Winnipeg, Canada. From 1997 to 2003, and from 2009 to 2012 he was the Director of the International Centre for Human Rights & Democratic Development (later, Rights and Democracy). He was a member of the Canadian delegation to the UN General Assembly (1980), a member of the Canadian delegation to the UN Conference on an International Criminal Court (1998), and a member of the Canadian Delegation to the International Forum on the Holocaust Stockholm (2000), Prague 2007, Linz and Vienna 2008. He has been a frequent member of the Canadian delegation to the Organization on Security and Cooperation in Europe Conferences on Anti-Semitism and Intolerance (Vienna 2003, Berlin 2004, Bucharest 2007). In 2005, he authored the book *Aftershock: Anti-Zionism and Antisemitism*, published by Dundurn. In 2013, he co-authored *Online Antisemitism: A Systematic Review of the Problem, the Response and the Need for Change*, a report published by Israel's Global Forum for Combating Antisemitism.

Erez Padan
is an advocate who has worked at the State Attorney Office of Israel since 1999. His positions in the Jerusalem District Attorney Office include senior prosecutor, team leader and department director. Since 2015, he has headed a department of prosecutors that handles all cases in which defendants are held in custody during trial, directing the preparation of cases and authorizing indictments. In this capacity, he plays a central role in Israel's enforcement efforts against incitement. During 2015–2016, his office issued over thirty indictments for various forms of criminal incitement, including those involving social media. His office has gained significant experience in handling incitement cases and the associated evidentiary and other legal issues.

Sylvie Schlanger
is an advocate-general and assistant of the general Prosecutor of the Paris Court of Appeal. She specializes in criminal fields such as cybercrime, civil and criminal cases and terrorism incriminations. She previously taught criminal

law at the Sorbonne University in Paris. She has over thirty years experience as a prosecutor. She has also served in the civil service and worked for the general magistracy inspectorate.

Ronald Thwaites, QC

originally forged a career as a defense advocate in major criminal cases of all kinds, including Irish terrorism cases. He later made a transition to civil work, including defamation and media work as well as often acting in health and safety cases for commercial corporations. He also defended three Commissioners of the Metropolitan Police in two major pubic inquiries and for a number of health and safety breaches including one arising from the shooting dead of an innocent man, (Jean-Charles de Menezes) who was mistaken for a terrorist. He also appeared for several constabularies in malicious prosecution actions and inquests arising from deaths in custody. Over a period spanning two decades, he was known to have appeared in more libel jury trials than anyone else at the bar. In 2009, he was awarded the "Defamation Silk of the Year" award by Chambers Directory Awards. He was called to the bar in 1970, and made a QC in 1987.

Rachel VanLandingham

is an associate professor of law at Southwestern Law School in Los Angeles, CA. She was appointed after serving in the U.S. Air Force for over 20 years, including more than a decade as a Judge Advocate. She retired in the rank of Lieutenant Colonel. From 2006–2010 she served as the legal advisor for international law at Headquarters, U.S. Central Command, where she advised on operational and international legal issues related to the armed conflicts in Afghanistan and Iraq. She also served as the Command's Chief Liaison to the International Committee of the Red Cross. She is the 2015 winner of the Benjamin B. Ferencz Essay Competition for her article, "Criminally Disproportionate Warfare: Aggression as a Contextual War Crime." She is the co-editor of *Military Operations: Law, Policy and Practice* (OUP, 2015), which details the operationalization of law across the spectrum of U.S. military operations.

Sean Watts

is a Professor at Creighton University Law School and an operational law attorney at United States Strategic Command in his capacity as a Lieutenant Colonel in the U.S. Army JAG Reserve. He is a Senior Fellow with the NATO Cooperative Cyber Defence Center of Excellence in Tallinn, Estonia. He is also a Senior Fellow with the Lieber Center for Law and Land Warfare at the United States Military Academy at West Point. From 2010–2016 he participated in drafting both volumes of *The Tallinn Manual on International Law Applicable to Cyber Warfare*. From 2009–2011 he served as a defense team member in *Gotovina et al.* at the International Criminal Tribunal for Former Yugoslavia. He is also a co-founder of the annual Creighton Law School *Nuremberg to Hague Summer Program* in international criminal law. Prior to teaching, Professor Watts served as an active-duty U.S. Army officer for fifteen years in legal and operational assignments including: Professor of International Law at the Army JAG School, Rule of Law Advisor to the Afghan National Army and Ministry of Defense, Chief of Federal Tort Claims, Trial Defense Counsel, Chief of International and Operational Law, Tank Company Executive Officer, and Tank Platoon Leader in a U.S. Army Tank Battalion.

Introduction

Incitement to terrorism connects the dots between evil words and evil deeds. Hate precedes terror. History has already taught us that incitement to genocide and to crimes against humanity unchecked will inevitably bring devastation to humankind. Incitement is an affront to the dignity of its victims, and poses a dire threat to all people of good will.

Today, however, there is a new urgency to confront a malady that has found fresh ways to take root and multiply. A seemingly boundless array of communications options is now available for terrorists and their supporters to promote, inspire, catalyze – incite – violence against innocents.

Combating incitement to terrorism poses operational, constitutional and human rights challenges on many fronts, both domestically and internationally. What is incitement? Where should the line be drawn between protected speech and incitement that should be criminalized? Does war change the calculus of what are appropriate and lawful measures to contain and respond to such incitement? And, perhaps most challenging of all, how does social media and the nature of communication and engagement in today's virtual world change or complicate how we think about and can respond to incitement?

This compilation offers expert analysis on incitement to terrorism across these challenging issues and questions, and is based on presentations at a workshop held in December 2016 on 'Incitement to Terrorism' in New York City. The contributors bring expertise from a range of countries and operational experience, providing an illuminating and thought-provoking examination of domestic and international law, comparative approaches, operational perspectives and emerging trends with respect to incitement to terrorism.

The first part, "Foundational Issues," presents an important framework for the discussions, with essays focused on domestic and regional approaches to incitement to terrorism, state responsibility in the cyber arena, and the fundamental interplay between incitement and free speech protections. The second part, "Comparative Perspectives," examines the treatment of incitement in the domestic legal regimes of France, the United Kingdom, Canada, and Israel through contributions emanating from both individual authors and the workshop interchange. It also includes an international organization perspective centered on the UN. The third part, "Incitement, Terrorism and War," highlights the potential tools available during armed conflict for preventing or responding

* We wish to express our gratitude to David Litman and Sarah Willig in the preparation of this manuscript.

 | DOI 10.1163/9789004359826_002

to incitement, as well as key interpretive and analytical questions inherent in decision-making in wartime. Finally, the "Emerging Issues and Challenges" part tackles head-on the dangers of social media in the arena of incitement and possible avenues for combatting that threat, along with an interesting examination of the role of policing in addressing the threat of incitement.

It is our hope that this publication will be a useful and engaging tool for practitioners and scholars alike in grappling with the legal, ethical, operational and policy issues and conundrums that efforts to combat incitement to terrorism face on a daily basis and across many jurisdictions.

We gratefully acknowledge the contribution of the Pratt Foundation for making the workshop and this collection possible.

PART 1

Foundational Issues

Freedom of Expression, Hate Speech, and Incitement to Terrorism and Genocide: Resonances and Tensions

Gregory S. Gordon

1 Introduction

What is the relationship between international human rights law and domestic laws that strive to protect free speech while regulating hate speech, and incitement to terrorism and genocide? Examining the interplay between and among these different legal regimes demonstrates that international and domestic approaches to regulating hate speech and incitement help inform our general notions of the human rights boundaries regarding speech regulation. The policy and enforcement lessons are invaluable for any effective approach to criminalizing incitement to genocide and incitement to terrorism. The former has already been developed with those lessons in mind, but the latter is at an early stage. In addition, although incitement to genocide superficially differentiates itself from incitement to terrorism in certain obvious ways – most importantly the discriminatory-liquidation bent of genocide versus terrorism's intimidation-for-political gain focus, they actually share much in common. This is true upon deeper consideration of each delict's elements, overall objectives, enforcement priorities, and rhetorical techniques.

Given these resonances, development of incitement to terrorism could benefit greatly from the jurisprudential wisdom that has accumulated around incitement to genocide. In turn both of these speech-offense branches are helpfully contextualized, from doctrinal and policy perspectives, by international human rights and domestic laws. This paper will examine how these legal regimes, different in many important respects but also inextricably linked in certain others, interact with and influence one another.

The paper is divided into five parts. Part 2 below considers the human rights body of law by focusing on the International Covenant on Civil and Political Rights and the European Convention on Human Rights as a useful starting point, including an examination of the tests that have been developed under them, because they have particular relevance for incitement to terrorism. Next, in exploring the relationship between those instruments and domestic law approaches to speech, Part 3 focuses on the United States, with its extreme

 | DOI 10.1163/9789004359826_003

embrace of free speech, versus the balance of the liberal democracies of the world, which seek to balance that freedom with protection of dignity and multiculturalism. As is well known, the U.S. has a fairly exceptional stance on speech. In linking this analysis to incitement to terrorism, Part 4 examines the international efforts that have been made to criminalize it, as well as the interplay and differences between certain European domestic laws and U.S. law. Finally, Part 5 compares incitement to terrorism with incitement to genocide, highlighting some differences but mostly affirming many doctrinal and policy similarities.

2 The Human Rights Instruments and Regulation of Hate Speech

2.1 *Background*

By way of background, modern human rights instruments related to speech begin with the 1948 Universal Declaration of Human Rights. Article 19 provides for freedom of expression, but is somewhat in tension with Article 7, which provides for equality and states that incitement is prohibited.[1] That tension is reproduced in the 1953 European Convention on Human Rights in Article 10, which also guarantees freedom of expression but then has a "clawback" clause, which provides for limitations on it.[2] The 1966 International Convention on Elimination of Racial Discrimination from 1965 has an anti-incitement provision related to racial incitement at Article 4,[3] and then the International Covenant on Civil and Political Rights has the same tension built into its Article 19 as Article 10 did of the European Convention. However, the ICCPR also has a separate incitement provision in Article 20(2).[4] The ICCPR and the European Convention, as well as the tests that have been developed under them, form the foundation for the instant analysis.

2.2 *The International Covenant on Civil and Political Rights* (*ICCPR*)

Article 19(2) of the ICCPR enshrines the right to freedom of expression, but also contains a clawback clause under Subsection 3. That clause states: "The

1 General Assembly resolution 217(III) A, *Universal Declaration of Human Rights*, A/RES/217(III) A (10 December 1948), arts. 7, 19, http://www.un.org/en/ga/search/view_doc.asp?symbol=A/RES/217(III).

2 European Convention for the Protection of Human Rights and Fundamental Freedoms, art. 10, September 3, 1955, 213 U.N.T.S. 222.

3 International Convention on the Elimination of All Forms of Racial Discrimination, preface, January 4, 1969, 660 U.N.T.S. 195.

4 International Covenant on Civil and Political Rights, arts. 19, 20, March 23, 1976, 999 U.N.T.S. 171.

exercise of the rights provided for in paragraph two of this article carries with it special duties and responsibilities. It may therefore be subject to certain restrictions, but these shall only be such as are provided by law and are necessary for respect of the rights or reputations of others under A, and then under B, for the protection of national security or of public order, orde publique, or of public health or morals."

Article 20, on the other hand, addresses incitement in Subsection 2, which states that any advocacy of national, racial, or religious hatred that constitutes incitement to discrimination, hostility, or violence shall be prohibited by law. The juxtaposition and relationship among Article 19, Article 19(3) and Article 20(2) raises some interesting questions. The jurisprudence developed under Optional Protocol 1 to the ICCPR, which establishes an individual complaint procedure,[5] provides some answers.

More specifically, there are three cases of particular relevance, all dealing with anti-Semitic hate speech. In *J.R.T. & the W.G. Party vs. Canada* (1983), a white supremacist political party leader claimed Article 19 violations when the government cut off his access to a telephone line being used to disseminate tape-recorded anti-Semitic messages.[6] In *Faurisson vs. France* (1996), the complainant was a well-known Holocaust denier. He challenged his conviction in France for disseminating Holocaust denial speech as a violation of his Article 19 right to free expression.[7] And in *Ross vs. Canada* (2000), the school teacher complainant challenged a work reassignment based on his lessons on anti-Semitism in the classroom. He also brought his case before the Human Rights Committee under Article 19, claiming his right to freedom of expression was violated.[8]

How did the Human Rights Committee handle the interplay between Article 19 and Article 20? *Ross* disposed of the case pursuant to Article 19(3) and its clawback clause. In particular, the analysis was filtered through a three-part test. First, the Committee found that the restriction was provided by law – a legal framework was in place for the proceedings that resulted in Ross's reassignment. Second, it addressed one of the aims of Article 19(3); in this case,

5 Optional Protocol to the International Covenant on Civil and Political Rights, March 23, 1976, 999 U.N.T.S. 302.

6 International Covenant on Civil and Political Rights, Communication No. 104/1981: Canada (Jurisprudence), UN Doc. CCPR/C/18/D/104/1981 (*J.R.T. & the W.G. Party v. Canada*) (declared inadmissible April 6, 1983).

7 International Covenant on Civil and Political Rights, Communication No. 550/1993: France (Jurisprudence), UN Doc. CCPR/C/58/D/550/1993 (1996) (*Robert Faurisson v. France*).

8 International Covenant on Civil and Political Rights, Communication No. 736/1997: Canada (Jurisprudence) ¶ 2.1, UN Docs. CCPR/C/70/D/736/1997 (2000) (*Ross v. Canada*).

protecting the rights and reputations of the Jewish students. Third, the Human Rights Committee found that the restriction was necessary to achieve a legitimate purpose, again, to protect the rights or reputations of those students of the Jewish faith. So we see the use of a balancing test here. And this will be important when incitement to terrorism is considered later.

In contrast, the Human Rights Committee took a different approach in the other two cases, *J.R.T.* and *Faurisson*, relying on Article 20(2). In both cases, the Committee impliedly found that there was no violation of the Article 19(1) right to freedom of expression because the Canadian government's actions were necessitated pursuant to Article 20(2), the incitement provision.

2.3 *European Convention on Human Rights* (ECHR)

The same tension replicates itself in Article 10 of the European Convention on Human Rights. Article 10(1) provides for freedom of expression generally, but then Subsection 2 is the ECHR's clawback clause. It sets out duties and responsibilities that could be subject to such formalities, conditions, restrictions, or penalties as are prescribed by law. In particular, this provision is concerned with limitations on free speech "prescribed by law and necessary in a democratic society."[9] These are important terms, as the jurisprudence demonstrates.

Another limitation is "in the interest of national security," which is particularly relevant because of the focus on incitement to terrorism. "Territorial integrity or public safety" are also grounds for limitations, as are "prevention of disorder or crime." In addition, other restrictions are justified "for the protection of health or morals; for the protection of the reputation or the rights of others; for preventing the disclosure of information received in confidence; or for maintaining the authority and impartiality of the judiciary." So there is a fairly lengthy list of duties that go with the right that is articulated in Article 10(1).

Similarly, the European Court of Human Rights, which adjudicates cases that are litigated under the Convention, has put forth a balancing test similar to that laid out by the Human Rights Committee. It tries to strike the right balance between protecting the free speech right guaranteed by Article 10(1) and the government's prerogative to restrict that right to protect individuals as well as the various national interests just considered.

And the Court has found an equilibrium by applying a three-part test. First, are the restrictions prescribed by law (this is somewhat similar to the threshold inquiry considered in the Human Rights Committee cases)? Second, is their aim legitimate? And third – perhaps the most significant prong – can the restrictions be considered "necessary in a democratic society?" In turn, this

9 European Convention for the Protection of Human Rights and Fundamental Freedoms, art. 10(2), September 3, 1953, 213 U.N.T.S. 222.

latter inquiry tends to boil down to whether there is a "pressing social need" and an "intervention proportionate to the legitimate aims pursued."[10]

With that framework in mind, it is instructive to look at one of the critical judicial opinions illustrating it, *Zana vs. Turkey* (1997).[11] In that case, the complainant was a former mayor and supporter of the Kurdistan Workers Party (PKK), which was considered a terrorist organization. He told a journalist, "I support the PKK National Liberation movement; on the other hand, I am not in favor of massacres."[12] So there was some mitigating language in the comments. Zana also said: "Anyone can make mistakes, and the PKK killed women and children by mistake."[13] A Turkish court found that, when considered in the full context, Zana's rhetoric violated the criminal code's prohibition on public incitement to hatred and hostility. This finding was then challenged in the European Court of Human Rights. And with regard to the Article 10(2) test, the Court found that prongs one and two were easily satisfied. (This is true in most cases – there is typically no problem finding the appropriate law and the public safety motivation – the most litigated issue tends to be prong three.)

With respect to prong three, the Court parsed Zana's statements to determine if the restriction was necessary in a democratic society. And although there was some ambiguity in his statements, Zana seemingly provided justification for the PKK massacres. And, in this sense, context is key, and intent is also quite important. Here, Zana's identity was significant. He was a former mayor in this region in southeast Turkey and his statements coincided with massacres that were carried out by the PKK against civilians in that area. The Court found that his statements were likely to exacerbate an already explosive situation. As a result, it found that the restrictions could be proved as necessary in a democratic society, and therefore upheld the conviction. In doing so, it stated that Zana's conviction arose from a pressing social need and was proportionate to a legitimate aim.

3 Domestic Law Approaches to Regulating Hate Speech

What about domestic law approaches? Most liberal democracies focus on human dignity as an important right and therefore are willing to restrict speech

10 Jersild v. Denmark, App. 15890/89, Eur.Ct.H.R. (ser. A) 298, ¶¶ 29, 31 (1994), http://hudoc.echr.coe.int/eng?i=001-57891.

11 Zana v. Turkey, App. 18954/91, 1997-VII Eur.Ct.H.R. 2533, ¶12 (1997), http://hudoc.echr.coe.int/eng?i=001-58115.

12 *Id.*

13 *Id.*

to protect it. Canada takes a middle-ground approach. It has strong free speech guarantees, but does put an emphasis on dignity and also on multiculturalism, which is a unique aspect of Canada's ethos regarding regulation of speech.

And then there is the United States, the most speech-protective country in the world. The First Amendment to the US Constitution is absolute, providing, in relevant part: "Congress shall make no law … abridging the freedom of speech."[14] The US Supreme Court has interpreted this quite strictly, which has some important implications. One of them, among many, is the fact that although it is a party to the ICCPR, the United States made a reservation under Article 20.

This reservation was necessary given the US standard for addressing incitement, as established in the seminal case of *Brandenburg vs. Ohio* (1969).[15] *Brandenburg* replaced the "clear and present danger test," which was more permissive of speech regulation. In *Brandenburg*, the Court overturned the conviction of a Ku Klux Klan leader under an Ohio incitement law. The defendant had made threatening remarks regarding Jews and African-Americans, including "bury the niggers" while burning a cross at a Klan rally. The court held: "[Constitutional] guarantees of free speech and free press do not permit a State to forbid or proscribe advocacy of the use of force or of law violation, except where such advocacy is directed to inciting or producing imminent lawless action and is likely to incite or produce such action."[16] This is the world's strictest test in terms of regulating incitement.

4 International and Domestic Approaches to Incitement to Terrorism

4.1 *International Approaches*

Any examination of how the above domestic law approaches affect laws related to incitement to terrorism must begin with the international instruments that deal with this crime: the 2005 Council of Europe Convention on the Prevention of Terrorism[17] and U.N. Security Council Resolution 1624, also from 2005.[18]

---

14 U.S. CONST. amend I.

15 *Brandenburg v. Ohio*, 395 U.S. 444 (1969).

16 *Brandenburg*, 395 U.S. 444, 447.

17 Council of Europe Convention on the Prevention of Terrorism, art. 5, May 16, 2005, C.E.T.S. 196, http://conventions.coe.int/Treaty/en/Treaties/html/196.htm.

18 Security Council resolution 1624, *Threats to international peace and security*, S/RES/1624 (September 14, 2005), http://undocs.org/s/res/1624(2005), op. 1. Of note, it was the United Kingdom that moved for the Council of Europe instrument, and then pushed for a similar instrument at the United Nations as well.

Article 5 of the Council of Europe Convention obliges members to adopt such measures as may be necessary to criminalize public provocation to commit a terrorist offense as defined in Paragraph 1, when committed unlawfully and intentionally. Security Council Resolution 1624, which followed on its heels, then calls upon all states to adopt such measures as may be necessary and appropriate and in accordance with their obligations under international law to criminalize incitement to commit a terrorist act or acts.

A key difference in the language between the Convention and the Security Council Resolution is that the latter only deals with "acts" of terrorism. Here, the influence of the United States on the final formulation of the U.N. Security Council Resolution is evident. Of course, the United States had no role in the Council of Europe Convention. As a permanent member of the Security Council, however, it was able to exert its influence when Resolution 1624 was being debated in that body, because the other countries wanted the United States to sign on.

For example, in the more encompassing European instrument, the operative language requires states to criminalize glorification of terrorism (praising past acts), among other related activities – a result that would be anathema to the United States. As a result, the Security Council Resolution includes only hortatory language with respect to glorification in the preamble, but no operative language in the text of the resolution itself, undoubtedly a manifestation of U.S. influence.

What about the "direct" element? The language here reads: "where such conduct, whether or not directly advocating terrorist offenses."[19] What does that mean by implication? It signifies that indirect language is chargeable, a result simply inconceivable in U.S. law. Indeed, the Secretary-General's interpretation of incitement to a terrorist act under Resolution 1624 is a narrow one. "Only a direct call to commit a terrorist act, and that is at least likely to result in criminal action"[20] is prosecutable. Under this stricter standard, prosecutors must prove a double intent: the intent to incite and the intent to bring about the terrorist act. In contrast, the intent element in the European Convention is facially single-layered. Paragraph 1 of the Convention states that "[f]or purposes of this Convention, 'public provocation to commit a terrorist offence' means

19 *Id.*

20 Security Council resolution 1624, *Threats to international peace and security*, S/RES/1624 (September 14, 2005), available from http://www.un.org/en/ga/search/view_doc.asp?symbol=S/RES/1624(2005), ¶ 1.

the distribution, or otherwise making available, of a message to the public, with the intent to incite the commission of a terrorist offence."[21]

With regard to imminence, the European Convention refers to speech that "causes a danger that one or more such offenses may be committed." Thus, provocation must only cause a general "danger" that a terrorist offense may be committed, a broad approach to imminence. A "danger" that a terrorist offense may be committed represents a much more liberal standard than *Brandenburg*, one that would allow prosecutors to bring charges with respect to a greater scope of offenses than set forth in the Security Council Resolution.

Nonetheless, the Council of Europe Convention does contain limits related to respecting free speech and other human rights. Per Article 12, "each party shall ensure that the establishment, implementation, and application of the criminalization under Article 5 of the Convention are carried out while respecting human rights obligations, in particular the right to freedom of expression, freedom of association, and freedom of religion."[22] Similarly, Security Council Resolution 1624 itself refers to the Universal Declaration of Human Rights and the International Covenant on Civil and Political Rights. Both instruments thus contain language reminding parties that they still have to respect human rights obligations.

One critical issue remains unresolved in both instruments: exactly what is the meaning of "terrorism"? Unfortunately, there is no universally agreed-upon definition. That said, the Secretary-General's 2005 formulation could be a good starting point. It states:

> [Any] action in addition to actions already specified by the existing conventions on aspects of terrorism ... [acts] that [are] intended to cause death or serious bodily harm to civilians or non-combatants, when the purpose of such an act, by its nature or context, is to intimidate a population, or to compel a Government or an international organization to do or to abstain from doing any act.[23]

This boils down to acts causing harm to civilians and that have a purpose of intimidating a population or compelling a government to do something or

21 Council of Europe Convention on the Prevention of Terrorism, art. 5, May 16, 2005, C.E.T.S. 196, http://conventions.coe.int/Treaty/en/Treaties/html/196.htm.

22 *Id.* art.12.

23 United Nations, General Assembly, *In larger freedom: towards development, security and human rights for all: report of the Secretary-General*, A/59/2005, March 21, 2005, http://undocs.org/A/59/2005, ¶ 91.

abstain from doing something. And, as the definition notes, there are a number of international conventions with specific prohibitions, such as the Convention for the Suppression of Unlawful Seizure of Aircraft (1970).[24]

4.2 *Domestic Approaches*

Consistent with the Council of Europe Convention, the European domestic approach is more liberal. In general, European domestic laws cover not only incitement but also glorification as the following table shows:

State	Provision	Brief description
France	Article 24 of the French Press Act of 1881	Punishes incitement and glorification of terrorism
Germany	Section 129 of the Penal Code	Punishes statements that approve of unlawful acts
Spain	Article 578 of the Penal Code	Prohibits glorification of terrorism and commission of acts tending to discredit or humiliate victims of terrorist offences or their families
UK	Anti-Terrorism Act 2006	Criminalizes statements that may be understood as encouraging or glorifying terrorism

All of these statutes criminalize incitement, but also go further and punish as well glorification or "approval of unlawful acts." The Spanish statute even covers humiliation to victims of terrorist offenses or their families.

Not surprisingly, the American approach is quite different. The possibility of an incitement to terrorism statute in the United States is not even in the conversation. Instead, the U.S. criminalizes knowingly providing "material support" to a foreign terrorist organization, per 18 U.S.C. §§ 2339A 2339B (2006).

For example, in *Holder v. Humanitarian Law Project* (2010),[25] the U.S. Supreme Court ruled that the non-governmental organization Humanitarian Law Project (HLP) was not allowed to provide legal and policy training and advice to the PKK (the same group in the *Zana* case above) and the Tamil Tigers, which were designated terrorist organizations. Although HLP only sought

24 Convention for the Suppression of Unlawful Seizure of Aircraft, December 16, 1970, 22 U.S.T. 1641, 860 U.N.T.S. 105.

25 *Holder v. Humanitarian Law Project*, 561 US 1 (2010).

to teach these organizations how to comply with international humanitarian law – a seemingly beneficial endeavor that may have contributed toward peaceful resolution of disputes – the Court held that this constituted the provision of material support to a foreign terrorist organization in violation of 18 U.S.C. §§ 2339A 2339B. Although the statute restricted HLP's free speech rights, the Court found this restriction constitutionally permissible because of the fact that assistance was being provided to a terrorist organization (even if it would, on balance, lead to good results for society at large).

This result shows the potential danger of the American approach, which actually appears to be more restrictive of speech in the long run. Instead, a direct anti-incitement law would be more effective. Such a proscription can be justified on many grounds, including protection of human dignity, national security, and public order. These are the very rationales that support the human rights instruments considered in the first part of this paper. This is preferable to less direct mechanisms, such as that used by the United States in the *Holder* case, because they incorporate balancing tests and are more transparent in terms of dealing directly with speech. Further, these direct-incitement to terrorism prohibitions also have an important expressive value, by informing us that society views incitement to terrorism as normatively indefensible. At the same time, they permit direct prosecution of a great ill – incitement to terrorism. From this perspective, the European approach is, on balance, more effective than the US approach.

5 Comparing Incitement to Terrorism and Incitement to Genocide

5.1 *Background*

To compare incitement to terrorism with incitement to genocide, the more traditional offense, including both doctrinal aspects and policy objectives, it is first important to consider the origin of the crime of incitement to genocide. Article II of the 1948 Convention on the Prevention and Punishment of the Crime of Genocide defines genocide as a series of acts, including killing and serious bodily harm or mental harm, committed with the intent to destroy, in whole or in part, a national, ethnic, racial or religious group, as such.[26] Article III(c) then criminalizes direct and public incitement to commit genocide.[27]

---

26 Convention on the Prevention and Punishment of the Crime of Genocide, art. II, January 12, 1951, 78 U.N.T.S. 277 [hereinafter Genocide Convention].

27 Genocide Convention, art. III.

5.2 *Differences*

One significant difference is where the two offenses are situated in international law. Incitement to genocide is codified in a global treaty – the Genocide Convention – and is an *international* crime. Incitement to terrorism, on the other hand, is embodied in a regional instrument (the Council of Europe Convention) and a Security Council resolution, both of which reference incitement to terrorism as a *domestic* crime.

Moreover, the common definition of the target crime of genocide is internationally accepted. In contrast, there is no international consensus on the definition of terrorism.[28]

The target crimes for each incitement offense are also quite different. The target crime for incitement to genocide consists of destruction of a certain group because of the group's identity. In contrast, with incitement to terrorism, the target crime is about coercion through terror. Thus, these two target crimes have quite different elements, even though they both entail severe harm to civilian populations, which will be discussed below.

The groups or organizations that commit these target crimes are also different. Genocide is traditionally government-organized, although an evolution in this regard is evident. ISIS, for example, is a terrorist organization – although it fancies itself a State – and has definitely become a genocidal entity.[29] Terrorism, however, is a crime traditionally committed by non-state entities. Recently, some states, such as Iran and Libya (under Muammar Gaddafi), are sponsors of terrorism, demonstrating that terrorism has developed a State connection.[30]

5.3 *Commonalities*

Despite these differences, there are important doctrinal and policy overlaps between incitement to genocide and incitement to terrorism. Those overlaps include: (1) elements; (2) enforcement objectives; (3) criminal objectives and (4) incitement techniques.

---

28 *See:* Jacqueline S. Hodgson & Victor Tadros, *The Impossibility of Defining Terrorism*, 16 New Crim. L. Rev. 494 (2013) (noting lack of international legal consensus on how to define terrorism).

29 Gerald Waltman III, *Prosecuting ISIS*, 85 Miss. L.J. 817, 837 n.110 (2016).

30 Alison Elizabeth Chase, *Legal Mechanisms of the International Community and the United States Concerning State Sponsorship of Terrorism*, 45 Va. J. Int'l L. 41, 49 (2004).

5.3.1 Elements of the Crimes

5.3.1.1 *Direct*

First, both incitement to genocide and incitement to terrorism generally require that the incitement be "direct." In other words, did the audience for whom the message was intended immediately grasp the meaning thereof?[31] For incitement to terrorism, U.N. Security Council Resolution 1624 similarly mandates that incitement to terrorism be direct. However, the Council of Europe Convention does not, so that law is developing and we can only say that the "direct" element is shared between incitement to genocide and incitement to terrorism as formulated in Resolution 1624.

5.3.1.2 *Public*

The fact that the incitement has to be "public" is true for both crimes. As we have seen, the European Council Convention criminalizes "public" provocation (even if Resolution 1624 is silent in this regard). Incitement to genocide jurisprudence affirms that the "public" element can be satisfied via transmission through mass media, in a large group, or in a public place.[32]

5.3.1.3 Mens Rea

For incitement to genocide, the *mens rea*, or the mental element, is double: the intent to incite and the intent to commit the target crime.[33] In comparison, the Council of Europe Convention only refers to "the intent to incite the commission of a terrorist offence." But Yaël Ronen points out that offense nevertheless carries a double intent requirement: the intent "that those incited carry out the actus reus of the terrorist act, and that the act intimidate a population or compel a government to act or refrain from acting in a certain manner."[34]

5.3.1.4 *Causation*

Both of these incitement crimes are known as "inchoate" offenses. In other words, the crime is committed when the words are uttered in the proper

---

31 Gregory S. Gordon, *From Incitement to Indictment? Prosecuting Iran's President for Advocating Israel's Destruction and Piecing Together Incitement Law's Emerging Analytical Framework*, 98 J. Crim. L. & Criminology 853, 872 (2008).

32 *Id.* at 881.

33 *Id.*

34 Yaël Ronen, *Terrorism and Freedom of Expression in International Law*, *in* RESEARCH HANDBOOK ON INTERNATIONAL LAW AND TERRORISM 451 (Ben Saul ed., 2015). But Ronen notes that double intent is not likely required under Security Council Resolution 1624 because it carries the "direct" requirement. *Id.*

context. There need be no resultant violence.[35] In other words, causation is not an element.[36]

5.3.1.5 *Incitement*

Regarding the incitement element, the International Criminal Tribunal for Rwanda requires an examination of the speaker's objectives for the crime of incitement to genocide – what is the purpose of this speech?[37] Obviously, news and similar speech would be patently legitimate. A direct call for violence, on the other hand, is certainly illegitimate. In many cases, the particular speech is situated in a twilight zone between these two poles and we will have to parse the text. In the absence of any jurisprudence regarding incitement to terrorism, it is logical to assume the "purpose" criterion would apply as well. For example, certain code words demonstrate such purpose – especially allusions to animals or vermin or pests and creatures of that nature, which represent an attempt to dehumanize. And such words should be flagged.[38]

The context in which the speech occurs is probably the most important. For example, has there been, or is there ongoing, genocidal violence or rhetoric? In incitement to genocide jurisprudence, the nature of the environment is critical to understanding the legal significance of the speech.[39] Again, it seems likely that a similar criterion would be considered for incitement to terrorism.

5.3.2 Enforcement Commonalities

There are a number of criminal enforcement commonalities between the two offenses. Preventing recruitment is one that applies to terrorism and certainly applies to genocide. Preventing radicalization is another one. Although "radicalization" tends to be considered strictly in connection with terrorism, on deeper reflection, it applies equally to genocide. To convince a population to commit genocide, that is, to slaughter thousands of innocent victims, individuals

---

35 Elizabeth M. Renieris, *Combatting Incitement to Terrorism on the Internet: Comparative Approaches in the United States and the United Kingdom and the Need for International Solution*, 11 Vand J. Ent. & Tech. L. 673, 682 (2009) (in reference to incitement to terrorism); Susan Benesch, *Vile Crime or Inalienable Right: Defining Incitement to Genocide*, 48 Va. J. Int'l L. 485, 494 (2008) (in reference to incitement to genocide).

36 GREGORY S. GORDON, ATROCITY SPEECH LAW: FOUNDATION, FRAGMENTATION, FRUITION 9 (2017) (noting that causation is not a required element and specifying that "to make out a prima facie case, the prosecutor need not prove the incitement resulted in genocide.").

37 *Id.* at 874–875.

38 *Id.* at 866–867.

39 *Id.* at 875.

must be radicalized. This is no ordinary conduct, and incitement is a necessary component.

Preventing commission of the target crime is clearly the most important enforcement objective,[40] as is punishing inherently dangerous conduct before the target crime can be committed. In fact, these goals are the essence of criminalizing incitement. Promoting deterrence and educating the public are also important enforcement goals for both crimes.

5.3.3 Target Crime Objective: Severe Harm to a Civilian Population

For each of these incitement offenses, the target crimes aim for severe harm to a civilian population. For incitement to genocide, we need only look at the Holocaust, when 6 million Jews were murdered, or the Rwandan Genocide, when up to 800,000 Tutsis and moderate Hutus were slaughtered in only 100 days. Genocide has also been committed on a smaller scale, with fewer people murdered. In Srebrenica, for example, approximately 8,000 men and boys were liquidated. In a patriarchal society such as Srebrenica, where nearly all the males were killed, that society was destroyed.[41] This is genocide in a qualitative sense, as opposed to viewing it from a strictly quantitative approach.[42]

Terrorism also inflicts severe harm on civilian populations. The most glaring example is the 9/11 attacks of 2001. Nearly 3,000 people were killed in one day.[43] At present, various terrorist organizations are attempting to gain possession of nuclear weapons that could result in millions of deaths.[44] So, clearly, extreme harm to the civilian population is implicated.

In fact, one might reasonably conclude that there has been somewhat of a merging between modern terrorism and genocide. ISIS, a terrorist organization that is administering territory, has a genocidal policy toward Yazidis and others;[45] Hamas, a terrorist organization that is currently governing Gaza, has

40 *Id.* at 854.

41 Tatiana E. Sainati, *Toward a Comparative Approach to the Crime of Genocide*, 62 Duke L.J.161, 188–189 (2014).

42 *Id.*

43 Eric Lipton, *Death Toll Is Near 3,000, but Some Uncertainty over the Count Remains*, N.Y. TIMES, Sept. 11, 2002, at G47.

44 James Kraska, *Torts and Terror: Rethinking Deterrence Models and Catastrophic Terrorist Attack*, 22 Am. U. Int'l L. Rev. 361, 366 (2007).

45 Arielle Mullaney, Note, *Wiping Out an Entire Religion: How ISIS Will Inevitably Eliminate an Ancient Culture Unless the United States Employs Military and Diplomatic Intervention*, 39 Suffolk Transnat'l L. Rev. 107, 120–122 (2016).

a genocidal policy towards Jews;[46] and Boko Haram, an Islamist terrorist organization in Nigeria, has a genocidal policy towards Christians and Southerners in that country.[47] So modern forms of terrorism can sometimes take on a genocidal bent.

5.3.4 Incitement Techniques

5.3.4.1 *Glorification*

And then there is overlapping in terms of incitement techniques. Both incitement to genocide and terrorism tend to glorify past violence. For example, glorification of terrorism is currently taking place in the Palestinian Authority (PA). A recent example would be Jabril Raboul, a PA official, possibly a successor to PA leader Mahmoud Abbas. In 2015, he called a shooting attack in Beersheba that killed two and injured eleven an act of heroism.[48]

This incitement technique has resonances with the Rwandan Genocide. In addressing the population on Radio Télévision Libre des Mille Collines, RTLM, the infamous "Radio Machete," announcer Georges Ruggiu congratulated the "valiant combatants" who engaged in a "battle" against innocent Tutsi civilians.[49] This was glorification of genocidal violence.

5.3.4.2 *Accusation in a Mirror*

Both offenses employ a technique known as "accusation in a mirror," which occurs when the perpetrator of the crime tries to accuse the victims of the very thing that the perpetrator is doing. It is an insidious technique, but was used to great effect in the Rwandan Genocide.[50] For example, in an infamous speech in the lead-up to the Rwandan genocide, Hutu extremist politician Léon Mugesera declared:

---

46 Alexander Tsesis, *Antisemitism and Hate Speech Studies*, 16 Rutgers J.L. & Religion 352, 354 (2015).

47 Genocide Watch, *Time to Recognize Genocide: Boko Haram Maintains Mass Killings in 2016*, February 2, 2016, http://genocidewatch.net/2016/02/09/justice-for-jos-project-and-us-nigeria-law-group-on-boko-haram-attacks/.

48 *11 Outrageous Examples of Palestinian Incitement*, THE TOWER, November 22, 2015, http://www.thetower.org/2596-11-outrageous-examples-of-palestinian-incitement/.

49 *Prosecutor v. Ruggiu*, Case No. ICTR 97-32-I, Judgment and Sentence, ¶44(v) (June 1, 2000).

50 *See:* Kenneth L. Marcus, *Accusation in a Mirror*, 43 Loy. U. Chi. L.J. 357, 358 (2012) ("In other words, AiM [Accusation in a Mirror] is a rhetorical practice in which one falsely accuses one's enemies of conducting, plotting, or desiring to commit precisely the same transgressions that one plans to commit against them.").

> "These people called *inyenzi*" [which means "cockroaches" thus also representing dehumanization] "are now on their way to attack us. I am telling you, and I am not lying, it is they who want to exterminate us. They only want to exterminate us. They have no other aim. Are we really waiting till they come to exterminate us?"[51]

This speech was delivered by a person whose organization was planning genocide. So this is classic accusation in a mirror.

Similarly, when Palestinian attacker Ibrahim Allan and his accomplice stabbed to death 24-year-old Shlomit Krigman and a security guard was then forced to shoot them to prevent further carnage, the stabbers were engaging in terrorism while the security guard was discharging his duty in conformity with the law. But Palestinians have used this as a vehicle for incitement through inflammatory rhetoric to the effect that the Israeli security guard was committing an act of terrorism.[52] And so, again, they turn reality on its head and engage in accusation in a mirror.

5.3.4.3 *Dehumanization*

A final, and critically important, incitement technique is dehumanization. After all, what does it take to treat fellow human beings as though they are not human beings? And the answer is this dehumanization technique. In genocidal Rwanda, extremist Hutus routinely dehumanized Tutsis by referring to them in their incitement as snakes, cockroaches, and rats.[53] Similarly, consider *Der Stuermer*, which was the viciously anti-Semitic paper edited by Julius Streicher.[54] Based on the content of his newspaper, Streicher was prosecuted for crimes against humanity and found guilty at Nuremberg.[55] The Palestinian Authority's outlets – and even children's shows and school curricula – have long called Jews snakes, monkeys, and pigs and called for the annihilation of Israel.[56]

---

51 *Mugesera v. Canada*, [2005] 2 S.C.R. 100, 2005 SCC 40 app. III, ¶18.

52 Tzipi Hotovely, *Palestinian Incitement: Hate-Speech That Kills*, NEWSWEEK, January 31, 2016, http://europe.newsweek.com/palestinian-incitement-hate-speech-kills-421424?rm=eu.

53 David Livingstone Smith, LESS THAN HUMAN: WHY WE DEMEAN, ENSLAVE, AND EXTERMINATE OTHERS 152 (2011).

54 Robert S. Wistricht, DEMONIZING THE OTHER: ANTISEMITISM, RACISM AND XEONOPHOBIA 226 (1999).

55 Erin Steuter and Deborah Wills, AT WAR WITH METAPHOR: MEDIA, PROPAGANDA, AND RACISM IN THE WAR ON TERROR 142 (2008).

56 *Case Study: Portraying Jews as "Apes and Pigs,"* PALESTINIAN MEDIA WATCH, http://www.palwatch.org/main.aspx?fi=786; Jewish Virtual Library, *Arab/Muslim Anti-Semitism: Muslim Clerics – Jews Are the Descendants of Apes, Pigs, And Other Animals*, http://www.jewishvirtuallibrary.org/muslim-clerics-jews-are-the-descendants-of-apes-pigs-and-other-animals.

6 Conclusion

Several golden threads, often in tension with one another, run through the legal analysis related to various efforts to regulate speech. First, freedom of expression is essential in any healthy democratic society. Serious efforts have been made to protect free speech in the area of human rights, domestic laws, and international instruments. That said, the law also places a premium on the notion of protecting human dignity (as well as multiculturalism). Laws designed to regulate conduct arising from this norm include restrictions placed on hatemongers wishing to spew their venom on an innocent and unsuspecting public. Incitement laws address this problem. In that regard, because the US lacks any laws restricting hate speech for content-based reasons (compared to other liberal democracies), outgroups in American society are vulnerable. Such hate speech can often become so severe that it is deemed incitement. Unless that incitement is geared toward creating imminent lawless action, and reasonably likely to do so, no law prohibits such weaponized words being directed toward outgroups in the United Sates.

Movement along the continuum between such modes of speech and incitement to genocide and terrorism can often happen suddenly and imperceptibly. The law has been well-developed in reference to incitement to genocide, but is only in its infancy with respect to incitement to terrorism. Although these two delicts might seem quite different at first blush, deeper analysis reveals important resonances between them. In terms of elements, enforcement, objectives and rhetorical techniques, these two crimes share much in common. In that regard, perhaps jurists and academics who deal with both offenses should be looking to the older offense while seeking to develop the newer one. Speech is both a catalyst and fuel for large-scale assaults on innocent civilians. Whether the goal is to eliminate enemies through concentration camps or via blowing up thousands of citizens at once, the speech that inspires the perpetrators can be studied as the lynchpin for, and foundation of, international crimes. Understanding and eradicating one might then lead to better understanding and eradication of the other. We must keep this in mind as we attempt to develop a comprehensive and effective approach to incitement law.

Public International Law and Cyber Incitements to Violence

Sean Watts

Cyberspace and the Internet have proven unrivaled in their capacities to link humans. Instantaneous and global means of exchange such as Twitter, Facebook, Skype, and WhatsApp satisfy basic desires to connect and collaborate with both like-minded and dissimilar persons and groups. The Internet and its various platforms are extraordinarily effective sources of personal, technical, material, and financial support to individuals' ideological and professional ambitions. In these respects, the Internet, though still in its relative infancy, may already be the greatest enabler in human history.

However, the Internet has proved to be an equal-opportunity enabler. Projects and ambitions, whether benevolent or malicious, productive or destructive, find an Internet willing and able to facilitate their pursuits. Just as a community organizer tackling youth delinquency can locate and inspire assistance and contributors, a burgeoning terrorist cell can recruit and cultivate members and accomplices. Just as an advocacy group can inform and inspire listeners with constructive and enlightened ideas, a hate group can sow the seeds of mistrust, hatred, and violence. Whatever understanding, compassion, and savvy can be gained from the Internet, it seems enmity, alienation, and ignorance can be gained in equal measure.

The challenge of how to preserve the free and open exchange of ideas while guaranteeing order and security is not new. But it gains perhaps a new sense of urgency in the age of super-empowered, hyper-networked malevolent non-State actors. Already, the power of small groups and even individuals to impose enormous costs and inflict serious damage by cyber means is clear. Controlling and mitigating hate and terrorist groups' capacity to leverage cyberspace toward violent ends is now an urgent imperative.

A wide range of governance options, private and public, domestic and international, legal and policy-based, present themselves as possible approaches to the problem of cyber incitements to violence. Issues stemming from regulation of hate speech and incitements to violence are by now well known to domestic constitutional, criminal, and tort law. And regional human rights regimes have made important legal contributions, especially toward leveling various national approaches into coherent, international systems of regulation.

 | DOI 10.1163/9789004359826_004

But perhaps as important as regulating hate and terrorist groups directly is regulating the States and State-hosted cyber infrastructure that facilitate their schemes. Although sometimes conceived as merely virtual or even metaphysical, cyberspace is an utterly physical entity. It is comprised of networks, nodes, servers, cables, and transmitters. And this infrastructure resides overwhelmingly on territory belonging to or controlled by sovereign States. Incitements to violence by cyber means will often have emanated from or transited through one or many more States' territory. In this respect, effective responses demand not only attention to networked hate groups themselves but also to complex State-to-State international relations.

Understood as a problem of international relations, cyber incitement to violence immediately involves a wide range of international law principles and disciplines. International law rules concerning the use of force, the principle of non-intervention, sovereignty, State responsibility, and the duty of due diligence appear immediately relevant to international aspects of cyber incitement to violence. Yet because each of these disciplines was conceived well before the advent of cyberspace, each requires sometimes subtle and sometimes drastic doctrinal adjustments to operate effectively in cyberspace.

Cyber incitements to violence, especially when conducted by States or State agents, implicate a number of primary rules – rules concerning conduct – of international law. The nature of a primary rule involved in a cyber incitement depends on the effects, and in some cases the purpose, of the incitement itself, but at least three primary rules regulate incitement to violence by cyber means generally.

The prohibition on the use of force in international relations is a fundamental and universally-recognized primary rule of international law. Although classically conceived as involving armed forces or other military means, the prohibition has broadened to include other activities as well. For instance, the International Court of Justice (ICJ) has characterized training and equipping armed groups for hostilities in another State as prohibited uses of force.[1] It is important to appreciate that the Court did not attribute the hostilities conducted by the groups in question to the State in order to find a use of force. Rather the Court characterized the acts of training and equipping themselves as uses of force. Cyber communications intended to inspire an armed group in another State to undertake hostilities against another State could easily be understood within the range of acts constituting use of force as understood by the ICJ. The Court has distinguished low-level or isolated violence from more

1 *Military and Paramilitary Activities in and Against Nicaragua* (*Nicaragua v. United States of America*), 1986 I.C.J. 14 (June 27).

grave uses of force.[2] But as experience with incitements to violence indicate, it is certainly possible for a cyber incitement to arouse violence on a scale sufficient to constitute a use of force.

A related, though more ambiguously constituted, rule prohibits States from coercive intervention in matters, internal or external, committed to the discretion of another State. The prohibition on intervention, or as it is also known the principle of non-intervention, is not clearly codified in any globally-binding treaty but is widely accepted as customary international law.[3] The classic case of prohibited intervention concerns a State's interference with the free functioning of another State's domestic political system. Choice of political systems, as well as many economic and cultural decisions, remain the near-exclusive prerogative of a territorial State. Outside interference to force change or actions the victim State would not otherwise undertake may constitute prohibited intervention. Not all interference with these matters is prohibited. To violate the principle of non-intervention, the interference in question must be coercive – it must force the victim State's hand. Still, it is not difficult to imagine circumstances where a State resorts to cyber means to incite groups in another State to effect coercive political, economic, or other change in violation of the principle of non-intervention.

Finally, the foundational principle of sovereignty offers a primary rule of conduct relevant to State incitements to violence. The principle of sovereignty lies at the heart of international law. It is the primary source of States' authority and especially their right to govern territory exclusively and independently from other States. No treaty addresses sovereignty exclusively or comprehensively. However, sovereignty and the requirement that it be respected is evident in nearly all international law rules and principles, including especially the prohibitions on the use of force and intervention discussed above. Violations of sovereignty that do not also amount to uses of force or interventions are generally regarded as less grave breaches of international law. But, under a majority view, they are internationally wrongful acts nonetheless. A cyber incitement that falls short of the use of force or that does not constitute a prohibited intervention might nonetheless be wrongful as a violation of sovereignty. For instance, cyber communications that cause mild unrest and violence that does not cause significant damage or threaten seriously the governmental workings of the target State may nonetheless constitute a violation

2 *Id.* at ¶191; *See also: Case Concerning Oil Platforms (Islamic Republic of Iran v. United States of America)*, 2003 I.C.J. 161, ¶51 (November 6).

3 *Military and Paramilitary Activities in and Against Nicaragua (Nicaragua v. United States of America)*, 1986 I.C.J. 14, ¶202 (June 27).

of that State's authority to govern affairs on its territory – a simple violation of sovereignty.

Beyond primary rules of conduct, international law offers secondary rules, such as the law of State responsibility, that are relevant to international incitements to violence. Secondary rules are often characterized as rules about rules. As distinguished from a primary rule, the law of State responsibility does not usually determine what is and is not wrongful under international law. Rather, the law of State responsibility identifies conditions under which legal liability for breaches of primary rules attaches in relations between States. The widely-accepted formula for State responsibility is: (1) an internationally wrongful conduct and (2) attribution to a State. Attribution of wrongful conduct is possible by several means. The following may be attributed to a State:

- acts by its organs;[4]
- acts by persons or entities exercising elements of its governmental authority;[5]
- acts by organs of another State placed at its disposal;[6]
- acts by persons or groups under its instructions, direction, or control.[7]

Thus, a broad range of theories of attribution is available to affix responsibility to States involved, even indirectly, in cyber incitements to violence. State responsibility also attaches for acts that aid or assist internationally wrongful conduct.[8] This form of responsibility is distinct from others in that it does not attribute the wrongful conduct to the aiding State but rather makes aiding or assisting such an act wrongful itself. In this respect, aid and assistance is more akin to a primary rule.

The principal significance of State responsibility is accountability. In international law circles, State responsibility is often envisioned as attaching for purposes of litigation. Where jurisdiction attaches to a tribunal, a responsible State can expect to be ordered to cease its conduct and to provide a remedy to its victim State. But State responsibility can be important outside litigation as well. Responsibility may be important legal capital in diplomatic negotiations.

---

4 Articles of State Responsibility, art. 4, 53 UN GAOR Supp. (No. 10) at 43, U.N. Doc. A/56/83 (2001).

5 *Id.* at art. 5.

6 *Id.* at art. 6.

7 *Id.* at art. 8.

8 *Id.* at art. 16.

More important perhaps, State responsibility can give a victim State the opportunity to resort to countermeasures.

Countermeasures are otherwise unlawful State acts that are lawful when undertaken to induce another State to cease unlawful conduct against it. Given the decentralized self-governing nature of international law, countermeasures are an important form of international law self-help. However, because of their potential to undermine international law, they are subject to important restrictions. First, they may only be undertaken to induce compliance by a State in breach of international law. Countermeasures may not be undertaken to punish. Second, only a victim State may resort to countermeasures. Third-party States may not undertake countermeasures on behalf of another State. Third, countermeasures may not rise to the level of a use of force. Use of force by States is restricted to self-defense and actions authorized by the United Nations Security Council.[9] Fourth, countermeasures must be necessary and proportionate to the international wrong that provokes them. And finally, countermeasures must be preceded by a demand to cease the unlawful activity that gives rise to their use.

Thus, a State that suffers cyber incitements to violence may characterize them as internationally wrongful and may resort to countermeasures when that incitement is attributable, through any of the various forms of liability, to another State – at least in theory. While wrongfulness may be easily established, attribution is notoriously elusive and difficult in cyberspace. Cyber means offer actors any number of techniques to mask their identity, to spoof others' identities, or to otherwise mislead or frustrate victims' efforts at accountability. State victims of internationally wrongful cyber acts face enormous obstacles establishing State responsibility. A State that suffers violence incited by cyber means but is unable to establish attribution to another State has not affixed State responsibility and therefore cannot undertake countermeasures. In practical terms, steps such as violating another State's sovereignty to shut down servers or any other measure amounting to an otherwise wrongful act would be largely unavailable. Absent the extraordinarily narrow circumstances of "Necessity,"[10] the victim State is faced with either accepting a disconcerting response gap or operating in breach of international law.

In part to address this State responsibility response gap, recent enthusiasm has developed for the notion of an international obligation of cyber due diligence. The principle of due diligence is not entirely new to international law. A 1949 case decided by the ICJ described something like due diligence when

---

9 UN Charter, arts. 2(4), 42, 51.

10 *See:* Articles of State Responsibility, art. 25, 53 UN GAOR Supp. (No. 10) at 43, U.N. Doc. A/56/83 (2001).

it noted "every state's obligation not to allow knowingly its territory to be used for acts contrary to the rights of other states."[11] Similarly, a 1941 international arbitral award between the United States and Canada observed, "no State has the right to use or permit the use of its territory ... to cause injury ... to the territory of another ... when the case is of serious consequence."[12]

At present, several doctrinal ambiguities surround due diligence but most of its proponents agree that the duty arises only with respect to known harm and a State need only undertake reasonably feasible measures to cease offending uses of its territory. Most also agree that there is no duty to affirmatively monitor networks or to prevent offending use of cyber infrastructure. Scholars have seized on due diligence as a promising way to ensure responsible and secure use of cyber infrastructure and to bolster peaceful and cooperative management of cyberspace by States.[13]

A less-appreciated advantage of applying due diligence to cyberspace, however, might be alleviation of the State responsibility response gap noted above. Consider the following: State A suffers cyber incitements to violence conducted by State B, launched from or routed through cyber infrastructure on territory of State C. Suppose the violence is sufficient to coercively influence political events in State A. Suppose further that State A is unable to determine precisely who is responsible for the cyber incitements. State A is only able to tell that the incitements came from infrastructure in State C. Under the law of State responsibility, although State A has suffered an internationally wrongful act, State A could not resort to countermeasures against either State B or State C because it cannot attribute the incitements. Recall that failure of attribution denies a finding of State responsibility making countermeasures unavailable.

If, however, an obligation of cyber due diligence is recognized, as the territorial State, State C could be responsible for failing its duty to cease harm emanating from its territory. If State A informs State C early of the incitements and State C, aware that its cyber infrastructure is being used to harm State A, does not terminate the incitements, State C is in breach of its due diligence obligation. State C's breach of due diligence constitutes an independent internationally wrongful act and State A may, subject to the limitations mentioned previously, resort to countermeasures against State C. In this sense, the duty of duty diligence mitigates against the response gap resulting from the failures of attribution so common to cyberspace.

---

11 *Corfu Channel (United Kingdom v. Albania)*, 1949 I.C.J. 4, 22 (April 9, 1949).

12 *Trail Smelter Case (U.S. v. Can.)* 3 Rep. Int'l Arb. Awards 1905, 1965 (April 16, 1941).

13 Scott Shackelford, et al., *Unpacking the International Law on Cybersecurity Due Diligence: Lessons from the Public and Private Sectors*, 17 Chi. J. Int'l L. 1 (2016).

But recognition of due diligence in cyberspace is not without drawbacks. Although an important aspect of self-help in the international legal system, the countermeasures that become available with breaches of diligence tend to undermine the international legal system because they themselves involve conduct in breach of international law. First, countermeasures condition States to think differently about international law. They subtly reduce the institutional and cognitive barriers against breach that internalized international law norms enjoy through regular observation and implementation. Countermeasures also incentivize development of means by which to breach international law. Second, in the way illustrated by the scenario above, recognition of cyber due diligence is likely to result in more frequent resort to self-help. In their underdeveloped state, norms for cyber diligence present fertile ground for allegations of breach. To paraphrase Geoffrey Best on the law of war during the first World War, due diligence might represent an "aid to vilification" rather than a meaningful restraint on conduct. Third, armed with the opportunity to address injuries from cyberspace through self-help, States may be reluctant to build or bolster more effective collective, multinational solutions. And fourth, by evading attribution for the acts in question and focusing simply on the fact of emanation or transit from State territory, due diligence misses the mark with respect to culpability. In the scenario described above, State B, the responsible actor, evades the countermeasures so long as attribution is frustrated. In short, by presenting more opportunities for more States to allege more breaches of international law, due diligence potentially increases the frequency of States' resort to countermeasures and their accompanying destabilizing effects.

We are still in the early days of cyber due diligence and, frankly, of the relationship between international law and cyberspace. There is some evidence that States are interested in refining international law to better address the threats posed by cyberspace generally and even cyber incitements to violence particularly. In recent remarks, U.S. State Department Legal Advisor Brian Egan observed, "all governments must work together to target online criminal activities – such as illicit money transfers, terrorist attack planning and coordination, criminal solicitation, and the provision of material support to terrorist groups. U.S. efforts to prevent the Internet from being used for terrorist purposes also focus on criminal activities that facilitate terrorism, such as financing and recruitment, not on restricting expressive content, even if that content is repugnant or inimical to our core values."[14]

---

14 Brian J. Egan, Remarks on International Law and Stability in Cyberspace, Berkeley Law School, (November 10, 2016), https://www.law.berkeley.edu/wp-content/uploads/2016/12/egan-talk-transcript-111016.pdf.

Whether and how to empower States to respond internationally to cyber incitements to violence is thus a pressing question. Preserving what is good about cyberspace, especially its capacity to connect far-flung people and ideas, while tempering its capacity to disrupt and harm international relations will obviously prove one of the most important challenges of the twenty-first century. Public international law offers important principles and doctrine to regulate harmful uses of cyberspace by States. However, careful attention to exactly how existing international legal doctrine should be applied or adapted to operate in cyberspace is less obvious. Initially attractive solutions, such as developing a cyber duty of diligence may contribute to short-term stability and offer attractive self-help options to States. Yet equal attention should be paid to the destabilizing and long-term structural costs of such solutions.

Incitement to Terror and Freedom of Speech

Micah Avni

I Have Experienced Radical Islamic Terrorism

I have experienced radical Islamic terrorism in a very personal way. My military commander was killed by the Hezbollah in roadside bombing in 1999; one of my closest friends was killed by Al Qaida onboard American Airlines Flight 11; and in October 2015, my father was brutally murdered by Hamas on a public bus in Jerusalem.

Spread of Terror

Nice, Orlando, Brussels, Paris, San Bernardino, Tel Aviv, New York, Moscow, Istanbul, Jerusalem and Mumbai. Once upon a time this list would have been associated with a geography class, but today, this list is part of a very clear and frightening pattern – radical Islamic terror is spreading like wildfire across the globe. This terror does not differentiate between religions, nationality, ethnicity, race or sexual preference.

If you have any doubt about the drama of this pattern, just type the words "list of Islamist terrorist attacks" into Google and click on the Wikipedia entry that comes up. The list is mind-boggling. If you plot the trajectory out on a graph, or pin the geographical spread out on a map, you will not be able to sleep at night. It is truly terrifying.

ISIS, Al Qaida, Boko Haram, Hezbollah, Hamas and tens of other radical Islamic terror organizations are tied together by a unified goal – Jihad, a holy war to spread radical Islam and overturn the core values in which our modern lives are grounded: freedom, liberty, equality, democracy, and social justice.

This is big stuff. It's not an academic discussion. It is life or death. The survival of the Western world as we know it. This is the backdrop to our discussion about incitement today.

Incitement on Social Media

The concept of Jihad, holy war against the infidels, has been around for centuries. So why is it spreading so quickly and so effectively now? The answer: social

 | DOI 10.1163/9789004359826_005

media. Facebook, YouTube, Twitter and tens of other social media companies have created platforms that allow poisonous ideas to spread, and evil people to communicate and unite in a massive feedback loop.

Jihad by the sword has evolved into "Open Source Jihad," where hundreds of organizations and thousands of terrorist leaders use social media platforms to incite, motivate, radicalize and instruct Muslim youth around the world, encouraging them to join in this horrific holy war. The open platforms of social media have become accomplices in this Open Source Jihad; allowing terrorist organizations, known terrorists and radicalized youth to operate freely for years.

Prior to the advent of the Internet and social media, incitement was not likely such a big legal issue. But with the technology to amplify messages, incitement has become a very real problem.

What is Incitement to Terrorism?

Incitement to terrorism is the action of provoking unlawful behavior or urging someone to behave unlawfully. In the US, the question of incitement is framed in terms of the Brandenburg Test: intent, imminence, and likelihood or predictability.

Palestinian Terrorism

Earlier this week, New York Times Jerusalem Bureau Chief Peter Baker wrote: "Facebook has become the battleground in a global struggle between free speech and incitement, and in few places is that more pronounced than in Israel, the West Bank and Gaza."[1]

So I would like to examine the question of incitement through the case of *Palestinian terrorism*. My home court, but just a small part of the larger problem of Open Source Jihad

1 Peter Baker, *Facebook Struggles to Put Out Online Fires in Israeli-Palestinian Conflict*, New York Times, December 7, 2016, https://www.nytimes.com/2016/12/07/world/middleeast/facebook-struggles-to-put-out-online-fires-in-israeli-palestinian-conflict.html.

Examples:

I think that we can all agree that if a person sits in a coffee shop in East Jerusalem and as part of the political discussion among friends says "Gosh, I hate Israel," that is not incitement.

I think that we can also agree that in case of a terrorist handler who spends weeks firing up a young recruit, poisoning him with hatred, and then, just when he feels that the recruit is ready to explode, says, "Tonight you should take a knife from your mother's kitchen, ride the bus to the center of Jerusalem and kill as many Jews as you can until you are shot by the police. And when that happens, please Allah, you will become a martyr, your family will be rewarded handsomely by the Palestinian Authority, parades will be held in your honor, and schools will be named after you. And, of course, don't forget about the 72 virgins waiting for you in Heaven." The handler is clearly guilty of incitement to terror.

There is a whole lot of gray area between these two examples.

Where Do We Draw the Line?

The question is: Where do we draw the line? Are we even plotting the line in the right dimension? What if my second example was not a recruiter, but Palestinian society itself?

Participation in the Ecosystem of Hate and Feedback Loop

With the growth of social media and connectivity, I believe the concept of incitement has evolved and we need to rethink our approach.

Incitement is not about a specific action, or statement or moment which brings about a specific result. Today, in the context of the spread of radical Islamic terror, and certainly in the context of Palestinian terror, incitement includes participation in the ecosystem of hate which is intentionally aimed at bringing about the likely result of terror – violent brutal murder with an endgame of genocide.

It is about participating in and strengthening the poisonous feedback loop.

In the Palestinian Authority, there is a well fed ecosystem of incitement to commit terror and destroy Israel. From nursery school, through the entire educational and extracurricular system, scouts, summer camps, sporting events.

By professional, religious and secular leadership. Post-terror encouragement – payments to families and the glorification of martyrs. All amplified by social media. All aimed at promoting terror and destroying Israel.

- When the nursery school teacher has children dress up in Hamas headbands and use toy guns to shot other children dressed up as Jews? Is this incitement?
- When the Palestinian Boy Scouts name their leadership program after the terrorist who murdered my father and tell children: to be a good scout you need to be like Bhaa Alyan (the terrorist who murdered my father), to go out and massacre innocent civilians. Is this incitement?
- When the principal of the high school in Jabel Mukaber invites Bhaa Alyan's father to speak and talk to the teenagers about the terrorist's legacy and encourages them to follow in his footsteps and kill Israelis. Is this incitement?
- When Beir Zeit, El Najach and Hebron universities organizes a readers' chain to glorify Bhaa Alyan and get his murderous message across. Is this incitement?
- When the Hamas Student Union produces and disseminates a video reenacting the brutal attack on Bus 78 where my father was murdered, and calls on people to do the same. Is this incitement?
- When the Palestinian Television replays a music video repeatedly which encourages children to go out and stab Jews. When they produce children's programing with this same message. Is this incitement?
- How about when all of these activities are posted, reposted and targeted at the same youth via social media? When they go viral? When people repost and retweet these materials with the intention of influencing others. Are they inciting?

Intent, Imminence and Likelihood

Does everyone involved in the activities described above intend for the children to grow up to become terrorists? Of course they do. That is exactly what they are telling them to do. It is their clear intention.

Do they know that these children are likely to become terrorists? Yes. They know for certain that some will.

They also know that most of those who do not become actual knife-wielding terrorists will support and applaud terror. And that they will certainly not speak out against it and will not act against it.

So is the result likely and predicable? I would argue that it is.

Is it imminent?

The ecosystem of incitement to radical Islamic terror is an ongoing, self-perpetuating phenomenon. It produces new terrorists daily.

How do we find ourselves with scores of children running out with knives to stab people in the street? They do not just wake up and decide to enact terror attacks. They are primed and motivated by the ecosystem I have described above.

The participants in the ecosystem of incitement to terror intend for it to result in terror and the destruction of Israel, the participants anticipate that their actions will result in murder.

As for imminence – Islamists have a different sense of time than Westerners. A long term view.

So, I would argue that *participating in the ecosystem of incitement to terror* ***is incitement***. All of the participants intend to create terror, they know that it will happen, and they know that it is ongoing. It will happen tomorrow, and again in a few days, and again few weeks later, and so on.

Freedom of Speech

Obviously, the key challenge to dealing with the ecosystem of incitement to terror is the issue of freedom of speech.

I think that the time has come to turn the question of freedom of speech on its head.

Hundreds of years ago, when the basic concept of freedom of speech evolved, it was still possible to have absolute control over public speech.

If the king did not like what someone said from their soapbox or pulpit – he beheaded them. If he did not like what came out of a printing press or publisher; he shut them down, and perhaps beheaded the owner for good measure too.

Information Today is Spread Freely, without Limitations

The internet, mobile connectivity and social media have changed all that. Today there are almost no limitations on how information and ideas spread. You can say, print and publish just about anything that you want and share it with millions of people instantaneously. For free.

Governments are hardly involved and social media companies do not really care; they actually encourage it in order to increase advertising revenue.

- *PewDiePie* – He is a 27-year-old Swedish fellow with almost 50 million YouTube subscribers, 14 billion views and was rated by Time Magazine as one of the 100 most influential people in the world. When he compliments a video game, sales go up. When he suggests people support a charity, lots of people contribute. If he had a political opinion, people would listen. Just yesterday he announced that he was unhappy with YouTube's new filtering algorithms – he felt they had changed them in order to give preference to an Indian-Canadian female YouTube personality so that she could become the most popular YouTuber and give the company a more multicultural face. They called him back immediately to discuss. It will be interesting to see how this plays out.
- *Recent US Elections* – One of the most fascinating issues around the recent election was "Fake News." Not only can you speak freely, you can lie freely on social media.
- *The Shadow* – A rapper in Israel, he spews hatred. He publishes daily on Facebook and has a following that is as large proportionately to Israel as Donald Trump's Facebook and Twitter following in the US. Quite scary. I would not say that he is inciting violence, but he is generating hatred towards Israeli Arabs and the left wing, and polarizing the nation in a very unhealthy way.
- *Jihadists* – Millions of posts, movies, etc. calling for adherents to destroy the West, destroy Israel, and carry out violent and deadly acts.

Slippery Slope

When I speak with friends and colleagues in the Western World about freedom of speech, I notice that they possess an almost "religious" belief on the topic – particularly in the United States. One of the core tenets is the *assumed slippery slope* – if we limit free speech just a bit, we will find ourselves in the next. Holocaust within moments.

Unfortunately, today we are experiencing the opposite effect.

The absolute freedom to express hatred is facilitating the spread of terror, polarizing the Western world, and perhaps setting the stage for an actual holy war with the proportions of a Holocaust.

Conclusion

So to summarize, I have two thoughts that I would like to contribute to this discussion:

- When thinking about incitement, we should take into account the ecosystem paradigm, which, in turn, will affect how we think about intent, imminence, and likelihood.
- We need to turn our thinking about freedom of speech on its head. Lose the slippery slope paradigm, and focus on the dangers inherent in the fact that any angry young man can spread poison virally to billions of people.

PART 2

Comparative Perspectives

Wrestling with Freedom of Expression and the Spread of Extremism: A UK Perspective

Ronald Thwaites

> Words can be like tiny doses of arsenic: they are swallowed unnoticed, appear to have no effect, and then after a little time the toxic reaction sets in after all.
>
> VICTOR KLEMPERER (1881–1960) *THE LANGUAGE OF THE THIRD REICH* 12 (2002)

∵

Freedom of expression is rightly regarded as a cornerstone of democracy but it is not, and never can be, an unfettered right.

In the UK, legislation limits the right to freedom of expression in circumstances where, among other things, racial hatred is likely to be stirred up. Part 3 of The Public Order Act of 1986 is one example. The sentencing provisions for stirring up racial hatred are set out under Section 27.3 of the Act, which provide that, on indictment, the maximum sentence is seven years imprisonment and a fine, or both. In the lower court, imprisonment is limited to a term not exceeding six months or a fine not exceeding £1,000. These provisions have, to date, not been extensively used in the U.K and when they have been and convictions followed, generally the sentences passed did not to reflect the seriousness of the cases.

At protests and demonstrations, historically, when the police have had to intervene to prevent a breach of the peace, protesters have been arrested, but often de-arrested, (released without charge) when the crisis of the moment has passed and things have calmed down. Typically, these regular protesters, (so-called "activists") have gone on to sue the police for compensation alleging false arrest. If, however, the protesters were prosecuted, it was usually under Section 4 or 5 of the Public Order Act, which resulted in them being bound over in the sum of £50 or £100 for 12 months to be of good behavior. If they refused to be bound over for threatening behavior as many of the activists did, they were sent to prison for between seven and twenty-one days. As a result, these offenses, sometimes involving incitement to violence and hatred by chanting

 | DOI 10.1163/9789004359826_006

slogans and holding up posters saying, for example, "Kill the Jews," have too often been dealt with as low-grade offenses that do not result in a significant prosecution or a prosecution at all.

A number of cases illustrate this point. In *Abdul v The Director of Public Prosecutions*,[1] a crowd of family, friends and well-wishers collected at Luton town center, when a regiment was returning home from having done service in Afghanistan and Iraq, and the soldiers were subjected to chants and banner waving from an opposing crowd of Muslims chanting that they were child murderers and rapists and that they should be ashamed of themselves for what they had done and that they would burn in hell. The protesters were arrested under Section 5, convicted, fined and appealed against their convictions, albeit, unsuccessfully.

On another occasion, an anti-Israel protestor, Naomi Wimborne- Idrissi attended Israel Independence Day celebrations with red paint on her hands, which she announced was intended to represent the blood of Palestinian children, distressing many people present. She was arrested, de-arrested and allowed to go without being charged. She sued the police for false arrest and her civil case dragged on and when the trial eventually came to be heard, she failed to appear. In the case of *R v Rogers*[2] the issue was whether the words "bloody foreigners" and "get back to your own country" were capable of amounting to a racially-aggravated form of a public order offence – the Court decided in the affirmative.

There have been cases in England where the Qur'an has been burned in public. In one of the cases, a copy was stolen from a public library and the event was recorded and then posted online. The defendant in that case was charged with the theft of a library book and sentenced to 60 days imprisonment, which was a pragmatic way of dealing with the problem, but raises questions regarding whether it was an appropriate way to deal with this type of offense when it was clearly intended to stir up racial hatred. In order to prosecute a person under Part 3 of the 1986 Act, the police must obtain the consent of the Attorney General; whether this procedural requirement is deterring them from prosecuting the more serious offenses is difficult to say.

Nonetheless, many commentators believe that the police, and in particular the Metropolitan Police Service (MPS), have been feeble in their handling of Muslims, particularly hate preachers such as Abu Hamza, tolerating conduct by them that they would not have permitted from other groups. Part of the reason may be found in the finding on "institutional racism" in the 1999

1 *Abdul v DPP*, [2011] EWHC 257 (Admin).

2 *R v Rogers* [2007] UKHL 8.

McPherson Inquiry into the murder investigation of Stephen Lawrence, the black victim of a racist murder.[3]

In common with many other countries, the UK has a number of well-known Muslim preachers. One of them, Anjem Choudary, was recently convicted under Section 12 of the Terrorism Act of 2000 for supporting a proscribed organization, ISIS, and endorsing their policy. He was sentenced to five and a half years imprisonment, (maximum sentence 10 years) but it took many years for the authorities to get a conviction.[4]

In Norwood v DPP,[5] the defendant displayed a poster in his window with a photograph of the Twin Towers in flames, with the words, "Islam out of Britain, Protect the British People." He was convicted on that occasion of an aggravated offense under Part 3, Section 19 of the Public Order Act, for stirring up racial hatred – but fined £300. The court said that it was a public expression of attack on all Muslims and a warning that their presence was a threat or danger to the British people which was clearly not acceptable. However, the low sentence imposed suggests that, on that occasion, the judge failed to use his sentencing powers appropriately.

On December 7, 2016, at the Central Criminal Court, Joshua Bonehill-Paine, a self-styled "nationalist, fascist, and supporter of white rights" was convicted of racially aggravated harassment (under the Protection from Harassment Act 1997[6]) against a member of parliament, Luciana Berger, about whom he published five vile articles online that resulted in 2,500 hate-filled tweets sent to her over the course of three days. He also made antisemitic attacks online including a picture of her face pasted onto a rodent with a Star of David on her head.[7]

---

3 William MacPherson, *The Stephen Lawrence Inquiry,* Report of an Inquiry to Parliament by the Secretary of State for the Home Department by Command of Her Majesty, February 1999, https://www.gov.uk/government/uploads/system/uploads/attachment_data/file/277111/4262.pdf.

4 David Anderson QC, Independent Reviewer of Terrorism Legislation opined that it was insufficiency of evidence rather than inadequacy of the law that allowed Choudary to remain active for so long. The Crown Prosecution Service (CPS) had considered prosecuting him on no fewer than 10 occasions between 2002–2015.

5 *Norwood v. DPP* [2003] EWCH 1564.

6 Protection from Harassment Act 1997, 1997 c. 40.

7 On December 8, 2016, Mr. Justice Spencer sentenced Bonehill-Paine to 2 years imprisonment, the maximum sentence for racially aggravated harassment to be served consecutively to his current sentence for hate crime, which may signal a change in sentencing policy in the UK for hate crime.

UK criminal law does not include a specific offense of a hate crime against an individual unless the act can be piggy-backed onto another offense. Instead, as first introduced by Section 145 of the Criminal Justice Act 2003, UK law provides courts with the authority to impose longer sentences on those who commit serious offenses that are racially aggravated.[8] As a result, there are many hate incidents that cannot be followed up by criminal proceedings unless the victims are also, for example, assaulted or threatened with assault or harassed.

There is a perpetual tension between freedom of expression and the need for society to protect individuals and groups from criminal activities of all kinds, including those motivated by hate and racism in all its forms. Although some believe that hate crime is punishing individuals for their thoughts, the law only intervenes when they turn their thoughts into unacceptable words or actions that cross the line into illegality. The UK has attempted to achieve a balance between the two, reflected in part in the terms of Section 29(j) of the Public Order Act 1986, a provision that allows for criticism of any individual's religion (or sexual orientation) as follows:

> Nothing in this Part should be read or given effect in a way which prohibits or restricts discussion, criticism or expressions of antipathy, dislike, ridicule, insult or abuse of particular religions or the beliefs or practices of its adherents, or proselytizing or urging adherents of a different religion or belief system to cease practising their religion or belief system.[9]

As Lord Justice Sedley said in Redmond-Bate v DPP: "Free speech includes not only the inoffensive, but the irritating, the contentious, the eccentric, the heretical, the unwelcome and the provocative ... provided it does not tend to provoke violence."[10]

Nonetheless, one should also consider those observations in the context of related observations by Lord Justice Rose in R v Saunders:

> One of the most important lessons of this century, as it nears its end, is that racism must not be allowed to flourish. The message must be received and understood in every corner of our society, in our streets and prisons, in the services, in the work place, on public transport, in our hospitals, public houses and clubs, that racism is evil. It cannot co-exist with with fairness and justice. It is incompatible with democratic civilization.[11]

8 Criminal Justice Act 2003, 2003 c. 44, s.145.

9 Public Order Act 1986, 1986 c. 64, s.29J.

10 *Redmond-Bate v. DPP* (1999) 7 BHRC 375.

11 *R v. Saunders* [2000] 2 Cr App R (s) 72.

Few people in the UK, outside of extreme right-wing groups, are inclined to criticize Islam at all because of the extreme and often violent reaction such criticism usually produces. One example, however, is the recent incident in which Louis Smith, an Olympic gymnast, ridiculed Islam in a video clip that (inevitably) appeared on the Internet. He and his friend received death threats. They apologized, met with Muslims and visited a mosque. In addition, British Gymnastics disciplined him by banning him from sport for two months, which cost him thousands of pounds in lost earnings. The decision was based on their code of practice which states: "Athletes may be ineligible for funding if they are derogatory about a person's gender, pregnancy or maternity, race, sexuality, marital status, belief, or age."[12] It therefore appears that sportsmen and women in the UK who wish to receive public funding do not enjoy the same freedom of expression as everyone else.[13]

The UK enacted new Terrorism Acts in 2000 and 2006. The main perpetrators of the most serious acts of terrorism are almost always charged with either murder, conspiracy to murder, or conspiracy to cause explosions. The Terrorism Act, as amended, broadened the definition of terrorism to apply to domestic terrorism and include any political, religious, racial, or ideological cause that uses or threatens violence against people or property to influence the government or any governmental organization, or to intimidate the public or a section of it.[14] It created new offenses of inciting terrorism, gave police enhanced powers, and increased pre-charge detention periods.[15] It also proscribed many terrorist groups, the list of which continues to grow, including extreme right wing organisations as well as Islamist ones.

The function of the Terrorism Acts 2000 and 2006 was to create a number of specific terrorism offenses to widen the net by extending the reach of the law to cover those who engaged in prior acts, encouragement, dissemination of terrorist materials, training, possession for terrorist purposes, and preparations. The boundaries of some of these offenses have not yet been tested. There have only been five prosecutions under Sections 1 and 2 of the Terrorism Act 2006 and the Home Office has admitted that such prosecutions are rare and far

12 *Statement: Louis Smith and Luke Carson Disciplinary Outcomes*, British Gymnastics, November 1, 2016, https://www.british-gymnastics.org/news-and-events/news/latest-news/6757-statement-louis-smith-and-luke-carson-disciplinary-hearing-s.

13 Matthew Syed, *Smith has lost thousands – just for using right to free speech*, THE SUNDAY TIMES, at 62, November 3, 2016.

14 Terrorism Act 2000, 2000 c. 11, s.1; *See also:* Terrorism Act 2006, 2006 c.11, s.34.

15 Terrorism Act 2000, 2000 c. 11, s.1, 40–53, 59–61; *See also:* Terrorism Act 2006, 2006 c.11, s.23–34.

from simple, with one particular challenge of the difficulty of explaining these sections to juries.[16]

What the 2005 London bombings (7/7) brought home to the UK was that the terrorist threat was at that time internal rather than external – three of the bombers were British-born sons of first generation immigrants from Pakistan and the fourth was an Islam convert from Jamaica. The UK authorities concentrated considerable efforts and resources on the "PREVENT" strategy,[17] which was designed to stop another generation from falling prey to violent extremism of the Al-Qaeda or related ideology. Since the war in Syria began five years ago, hundreds of radicalized young people, mostly men, have been to Syria to fight, and it is estimated that 450 have returned, of whom half are still committed to ISIS ideology.

In May 2015, the new Conservative government announced a new counter-extremist bill, followed by a separate counter-extremist strategy, in which it defined extremism as: "the vocal or active opposition to our fundamental values, including democracy, the rule of law, individual liberty, and the mutual respect and tolerance of different faiths and beliefs."[18] This definition has been criticized for being too general to provide a workable test for any new legislation. In addition, it leaves universities and others with conflicting obligations, since it has long been regarded as part of a healthy intellectual life at university to challenge orthodox ideas and introduce new initiatives that may be interpreted as undermining fundamental values.

In addition, non-Muslim faith groups have protested regarding any definition that would place them in jeopardy, such as some Christian groups who are hostile to homosexuality and fear that this definition therefore would – or might – affect them. In the joint parliamentary Committee on Human Rights, Counter-Extremism, Second Report of the session 2016 to 2017, the members reviewed past initiatives on trying to prevent the next generation from being radicalized and becoming extremists. The committee took evidence from experts and anticipated future developments, and in their summary stated:

16 Clive Walker described Sections 1 and 2 as "highly controversial" and "riddled with uncertainties and anomalies." Clive Walker, TERRORISM AND THE LAW (2011) at 8.155.

17 Home Office, *Prevent Strategy Presented to Parliament by the Secretary of State for the Home Department by Command of Her Majesty*, June 2011, https://www.gov.uk/government/uploads/system/uploads/attachment_data/file/97976/prevent-strategy-review.pdf.

18 Home Office, *Counter-Extremism Strategy Presented to Parliament by the Secretary of State for the Home Department by Command of Her Majesty*, October 2015, https://www.gov.uk/government/uploads/system/uploads/attachment_data/file/470088/51859_Cm9148_Accessible.pdf, at 9.

> The government's proposals for counter – [on countering ISIL-Deash-inspired terrorism] rest on the assumption that there is an escalator that starts with religious conservatism and ends with support for violent Jihadism, and that violence is therefore best tackled by curtailing or placing a restriction on religious conservatism.[19]

The committee expressed serious doubts about this approach, highlighting the problems of defining extremism and legislative gaps to be filled in this area. The government now proposes to put its counter-extremism proposals in the context of safeguarding potentially vulnerable people, but the detail is yet to come. It is perhaps unsurprising that the joint committee concluded that the UK government does not know what to do next on this issue.

---

19 House of Lords & House of Commons Joint Committee on Human Rights, *Counter-Extremism Second Report of Session 2016–17*, July 20, 2016, https://www.publications.parliament.uk/pa/jt201617/jtselect/jtrights/105/105.pdf.

French Law and EU Rules in the Fight Against Incitement to Terrorism or Violent Extremism

Sylvie Schlanger

1 Introduction

First of all I want to tell you, as we say in French: "la plume est serve mais la parole est libre." My speech is my own, and I am not expressing the opinions of the Parisian Court of Appeal.

After the November 13, 2015 Paris terrorist attacks, that left French citizens feeling horror and fear, the French government decided to strengthen counter-terrorism legislation, including the law of criminal procedure and the substantive criminal law. The changes have been completed and also subsequently amended.

France is a country that protects human rights, but the seriousness of the current terrorist threat has given rise to a special situation. The circumstances have led France to declare and expand a state of emergency in order to promote security as a priority, albeit at the expense of democratic practice and some human rights.

2 French Law

A fundamental French law of November 13, 2014 moved the offence of glorification of terrorism from the very permissive Freedom of the Press Act of 1881 (article 24), to the Penal Code in order to strengthen enforcement and extend the time limit for public action.[1]

Among other things, the time limit for court action was increased from a 3-month delay to a 3-year delay, starting from the date of the operative event. The motivation for this change is to reinforce a global response to these offenses and to protect public order.

The elements of this offence have not been modified, so the condition of public dissemination is still required.

1 Loi n° 2014-1353 du 13 novembre 2014 renforçant les dispositions relatives à la lutte contre le terrorisme.

 | DOI 10.1163/9789004359826_007

2.1 *Apology for Terrorism*

The offense of "apology for terrorism" refers to presenting or commenting in a positive way on a terrorist attack that has already occurred.[2] For example, the categorization as apology for terrorism would apply to a person who agrees with a violent and criminal assault perpetrated on innocent people in order to spread fear.

This offense must not be confused with revisionism of terrorist acts, which refers to denying the facts or claiming a conspiracy.

A qualification that needs to be satisfied for an "apology for terrorism" to have occurred is that the apology has be pronounced in public, such as during a public speech. This is the same rule that applies in France in the context of defamation or insults. An apology for terrorism can also be disseminated through social networks such as Facebook or Twitter.

The Paris Court of Appeal has defined apology this way: "apology presupposes a glorification or a justification of a criminal act or its perpetrator."[3]

According to the highest French court, la Cour de Cassation, the justification or glorification of the criminal himself or herself, (in the absence of some qualification or reservation), implies the justification of the criminal's crimes. So the glorification of the terrorist as an alleged hero would be considered the same as claiming there is a justification or approval of the terrorist's act.[4]

---

2 French Criminal Code, art. 421-2-5: "Le fait de provoquer directement à des actes de terrorisme ou de faire publiquement l'apologie de ces actes est puni de cinq ans d'emprisonnement et de 75 000 € d'amende. Les peines sont portées à sept ans d'emprisonnement et à 100 000 € d'amende lorsque les faits ont été commis en utilisant un service de communication au public en ligne. Lorsque les faits sont commis par la voie de la presse écrite ou audiovisuelle ou de la communication au public en ligne, les dispositions particulières des lois qui régissent ces matières sont applicables en ce qui concerne la détermination des personnes responsables.
Unofficial Translation: Art. 421-2-5. The act of directly provoking acts of terrorism or publicly defending such acts shall be punishable by five years' imprisonment and a fine of €75,000. The penalties are increased to seven years' imprisonment and a fine of €100,000 where the offense was committed by using an on-line public communication service. Where the facts are committed by means of the written or audiovisual press or the on-line public communication, the special provisions of the laws governing these matters shall apply as regards the determination of the persons responsible".

3 Unofficial translation. Cour d'Appel de Paris, 11ème chamber, Section A, Dossier N° 08/02208, JurisData: 2009-0011298, page 11, January 21, 2009 ("considérant que l'apologie suppose soit une glorification soit une justification valorisante d'un acte criminal ou de son auteur").

4 Cour de Cassation Criminal chamber, Criminal Bulletin N° 14, January 14, 1971, https://www.legifrance.gouv.fr/affichJuriJudi.do?idTexte=JURITEXT000007058993 ("La Cour de Cassation

As an illustration, on January 7, 2015, just after the terrorist attacks against the French satirical newspaper *Charlie Hebdo* and against the Kosher hypermarket in Paris, French comedian Dieudonné M'Bala M'Bala published a message on Facebook provocatively mixing the supportive message to the victims of the newspaper ("Je suis Charlie," *i.e.* "I am Charlie") with the name of the terrorist who attacked the Kosher hypermarket (Amédy Coulibaly). The French court referred to the message as a provocative amalgam and an apology for terrorism. M'Bala M'Bala received a two-month conditional imprisonment and 10,000 euros fine, confirmed on appeal, according to the law applicable at that time for this kind of offense (the Press Act of 1881).[5]

Note a divergence of view between the French Supreme Court and the European Court of Human Rights (ECtHR). The French Supreme Court considered the glorification of Maréchal Pétain – known for his support of the Nazi regime – to be protected expression within the meaning of the freedom to hold opinions.[6] In contrast, the ECtHR characterized the glorification of a man known for his support to the Nazi regime as an unprotected apology for crime against humanity.[7] The French Supreme Court distinguishes between the glorification of a person and the glorification of the criminal activities the person has supported.

a jugé que la justification d un criminel, en l absence de toute réserve, implique la justification globale de ses crimes.")

5 1881 Act on the freedom of the press, art. 23 (as modified by Act No. 2004-575 of June 2004 – Article 2 JORF 22 June 2004). Number 15012000640, JurisData: 2015-005323, Tribunal De Grande Instance Paris, March 18, 2015.

6 *Lehideux and Isorni v. France*, App. 24662/94, 1998-VII, Eur.Ct.H.R. 92 (1998) ¶23 (quoting the November 16, 1993 decision of the Court of Cassation: "In presenting as praiseworthy a person convicted of collusion with the enemy, the text glorified his crime and, in so doing, publicly defended it... In delivering that judgment, the Court of Appeal did not exceed its powers. Nor did it infringe the right to freedom of expression protected by Article 10, paragraph 1, of the European Convention for the Protection of Human Rights and Fundamental Freedoms, since the exercise of that right may, under paragraph 2 of that Article, be subject to certain restrictions prescribed by law, where these are necessary, as in the instant case, in the interests of national security, territorial integrity or public safety."

7 *Lehideux and Isorni v. France*, App. 24662/94, 1998-VII, Eur.Ct.H.R. 92 (1998) ¶47 ("[There is a] category of clearly established historical facts – such as the Holocaust – whose negation or revision would be removed from the protection of Article 10 by Article 17.53... There is no doubt that, like any other remark directed against the Convention's underlying values ..., the justification of a pro-Nazi policy could not be allowed to enjoy the protection afforded by Article 10...").

The punishment for an apology for terrorism has been significantly strengthened: the penalty has been increased from 45,000 euros to 75,000 euros and 5 years of imprisonment.[8]

The judge of expedited matters, to whom cases can be referred by the prosecutor, can stop a public online communication service that promotes information contrary to public order.[9] Even the reading of messages promoting information that is deemed contrary to public order may be repressed.

In addition, a law published June 3, 2016, defines two new offenses:

- The deliberate extraction, republishing or broadcast through the internet of an "apology" for terrorist acts (75,000 euros and 5 years of imprisonment)
- The habitual use, or consultation, of terrorist websites (2 years imprisonment).[10]

In a recent case, Jean-Marc Rouillan, the former leader of the terrorist group "Action Directe," called the November 13, 2015 terrorists "courageous" people. He was convicted of the offense of "apology for terrorism," and sentenced to 8 months imprisonment.[11] He has appealed the decision to the Paris Court of Appeal.

---

8 French Criminal Code, art. 421-2-5.

9 French Criminal Code, art. 706-23 (Modifié par LOI n°2014-1353 du Novembre 13, 2014 – art. 8, L'arrêt d'un service de communication au public en ligne peut être prononcé par le juge des référés pour les faits prévus à l'article 421-2-5 du code pénal lorsqu'ils constituent un trouble manifestement illicite, à la demande du ministère public ou de toute personne physique ou morale ayant intérêt à agir.).

10 French Criminal Code, art. 421-2-5-2 ("Le fait de consulter habituellement un service de communication au public en ligne mettant à disposition des messages, images ou représentations soit provoquant directement à la commission d'actes de terrorisme, soit faisant l'apologie de ces actes lorsque, à cette fin, ce service comporte des images ou représentations montrant la commission de tels actes consistant en des atteintes volontaires à la vie est puni de deux ans d'emprisonnement et de 30 000 € d'amende.") Unofficial Translation: 421-2-5-2: "Habitually consulting a public on-line communication service providing messages, images or representations directly causing the commission of acts of terrorism, or advocating such acts when, for this purpose, the service includes images or representations showing the commission of such acts consisting of deliberate violations of life is punishable by two years imprisonment and a fine of €30,000."

11 *Re Jean-Marc Rouillan*, No parquet: 16068000232, Jugement Correctionnel, Cour d'Appel de Paris,Tribunal de Grande Instance de Paris, September 7, 2016.

2.1.1 Provocation to Terrorism

Provocation to terrorism refers to direct incitement to commit terrorism, such as targeting specific people or places. It applies where the terrorist act has been planned in advance, but has not yet occurred. Any words, even when made to a closed group of people, or disseminated through a limited social network, are subject to criminal prosecution.

Article 421-2-5 of the French Penal Code reflects Article 5 of the Council of Europe Convention on the Prevention of Terrorism, which makes it an offense to intend to incite the commission of a terrorist offense.

Provocation to terrorism is punishable by imprisonment of 2 years and a fine of 75,000 euros. The penalty is increased by up to 7 years of imprisonment and a fine of 100,000 euros if the provocation to terrorism is committed through the Internet; the use of the Internet is considered to be an aggravating circumstance.

The French legal system has three particularly strong points for improving enforcement of terrorism offences:

- police infiltration operations can be allowed in terrorist cases by the public prosecutor or by a judge (considered to be independent and impartial in contrast to the public prosecutor who answers to the Ministry of Justice);[12]
- investigations under a pseudonym are permitted;[13]
- special rules for phone tapping and the interception of electronic messages or data.[14]

In addition, a special police department (Office central de lutte contre la cyber-criminalité) is empowered to close without delay any website disseminating messages to the glorification of terrorism.[15]

12 French Code of Criminal Procedure, arts. 706-81 to 70-687.

13 French Code of Criminal Procedure, art. 706-25-2.

14 French Code of Criminal Procedure, arts. 70-696, 706-97 to 706-97-6.

15 Loi n° 2004-575 du 21 juin 2004 pour la confiance dans l'économie numérique, art.6 ("Compte tenu de l'intérêt général attaché à la répression de l'apologie des crimes contre l'humanité, de l'incitation à la haine raciale ainsi que de la pornographie enfantine, les personnes mentionnées ci-dessus doivent concourir à la lutte contre la diffusion des infractions visées aux cinquième et huitième alinéas de l'article 24 de la loi du 29 juillet 1881 sur la liberté de la presse et à l'article 227-23 du code penal."); Décret n° 2015-125 du 5 février 2015 relatif au blocage des sites provoquant à des actes de terrorisme ou en faisant l'apologie et des sites diffusant des images et représentations de mineurs à caractère pornographique.

Users of on-line public services to which access is blocked are redirected to an information page of the Ministry of the Interior, indicating the reasons for blocking the site as a protection measure and providing the means of recourse.[16]

As an exception to the traditional rules, the Paris courts are specifically in charge of terrorist cases (the so-called "jacobin" structure). This means that even if the criminal offence occurs in another place (instead of Paris), special judges and public prosecutors of Paris courts have exclusive jurisdiction over these cases. Special police departments in charge of counter-terrorism such as RAID (Recherche, Assistance, Intervention, Dissuasion) and GIGN (Groupe d'intervention de la Gendarmerie nationale – the national counter-terrorism unit) are also based in Paris.

In 2015 a special database was created to register all people who have been convicted of a terrorism offense, and this file is centralized in the Paris Court of Appeal. 700 sentences have already been registered.

3 The European Directive

2.12.2015, COM(2015) 625 final, 2015/0281 (COD), Proposal for a "Directive of the European Parliament and of the Council"

In the aftermath of the terror attacks of November 13, 2015, a proposal was introduced for a "Directive of the European Parliament and of the Council."[17] The primary rationale of this proposal was to rebuild and reinforce internal security strategy.

The proposal has integrated important texts:

- Resolution 2178 (2014) of the United Nations Security Council[18] and the Additional Protocol to the Convention of European Council for Terrorism Prevention directed at foreign terrorist fighters;[19]

---

16 Décret n° 2015-125 du 5 février 2015 relatif au blocage des sites provoquant à des actes de terrorisme ou en faisant l'apologie et des sites diffusant des images et représentations de mineurs à caractère pornographique, https: //www.legifrance.gouv.fr/affichTexte.do?cidTexte=JORFTEXT000030195477&dateTexte=&categorieLien=id.

17 COM (2015) 625: Proposal for a Directive of the European Parliament and of the Council on combating terrorism and replacing Council Framework Decision 2002/475/JHA on combating terrorism, procedure 2015/0281/COD, http://eur-lex.europa.eu/procedure/EN/2015_281.

18 Security Council resolution 2178, *Threats to international peace and security caused by terrorist acts*, S/RES/2178, September 24, 2014, http://undocs.org/s/res/2178(2014).

19 Additional Protocol to the Council of Europe Convention on the Prevention of Terrorism, October 22, 2015, CETS No. 217.

- rules of the FATF (Financial Action Task Force) preventing the financing of terrorism.[20]

The proposal was presented in March 2016 by the European Commission to the Council; the Commission was required to deliver observations and modifications before negotiating parliamentary amendments.

The main purpose is to both reinforce existing offenses and to be one step ahead of terrorist attacks by criminalizing preparatory acts as proper offenses. For instance:

- criminalizing training abroad and travels to some areas of the world for terrorist purposes as well as incitement to commit such offenses. (Reports indicate that there are up to 5,000 people who have left the EU to undertake terrorist training and who have returned for the purpose of committing criminal offenses);[21]
- having a special regard for terrorism victims;
- asking Interpol, and other internal policy administrators, to cooperate and increase their forces to address terrorists' advanced skills in the use of the Internet and new communication technologies to disseminate propaganda, share knowledge and plan coordinated operations.

The 2015 proposed directive revises Council Framework Decision 2002/475/JHA (justice and home affairs)[22] and Council Framework Decision 2008/919/JHA of November 28, 2008 amending Framework Decision 2002/475/JHA on combating terrorism[23] three ways:

---

20 Financial Action Task Force , *International Standards on Combating Money Laundering and the Financing of Terrorism & Proliferation: The FATF Recommendations*, February 2012, http://www.fatf-gafi.org/media/fatf/documents/recommendations/pdfs/FATF_Recommendations.pdf.

21 Lizzie Dearden, *Isis: Up to 5,000 jihadists could be in Europe after returning from terror training camps abroad*, THE INDEPENDENT, February 20, 2016; http://www.independent.co.uk/news/world/europe/isis-up-to-5000-jihadists-in-europe-after-returning-from-terror-training-camps-daesh-islamic-state-a6885961.html.

22 Council Framework Decision of June 13, 2002 on combating terrorism (2002/475/JHA), http://eur-lex.europa.eu/legal-content/EN/TXT/?uri=celex:32002F0475.

23 Council Framework Decision 2008/919/JHA, amending Framework Decision 2002/475/JHA on combating terrorism, http://eur-lex.europa.eu/legal-content/en/TXT/?uri=CELEX%3A32008F0919.

- It adds the offense of travels for terrorism purposes (for foreign fighters);
- It adds the offense of funding and organizing these travels (furnishing means of transports, heavy weapons, trainings, and so on);
- It reinforces the right of the victims to be informed about procedures, and to benefit from both psychological and material help, including receiving emergency financial compensation.

The proportionality principle of Article 5 of the EU Treaty[24] means that the 2015 proposed directive is strictly limited to what is necessary and proportional. In other words, it proposes to cover all relevant conduct in accordance with the proportionality principle.

4 The European Court of Human Rights

Article 10 of the European Convention of Human Rights states:

Freedom of expression

1. Everyone has the right to freedom of expression. This right shall include freedom to hold opinions and to receive and impart information and ideas without interference by public authority and regardless of frontiers. This article shall not prevent States from requiring the licensing of broadcasting, television or cinema enterprises.
2. The exercise of these freedoms, since it carries with it duties and responsibilities, may be subject to such formalities, conditions, restrictions or penalties as are prescribed by law and are necessary in a democratic society, in the interests of national security, territorial integrity or public safety, for the prevention of disorder or crime, for the protection of health or moral, for the protection of the reputation or rights of others, for preventing the disclosure of information received in confidence, or for maintaining the authority and impartiality of the judiciary.

The rules of these principles are very clear, inspired by the ancient Greek democracy: even democratic leaders have to respect the supreme law and human rights.

24 Treaty of Lisbon Amending the Treaty on European Union and the Treaty Establishing the European Community, art.5, December 13, 2007, 2007/C 306/01.

In applying Article 10, the European Court of Human Rights has conferred a special status on journalists. In *Goodwin v. UK* (March 27, 1996), the Court stated that journalists are "watchdogs" of democracy because their job is to deliver verified information to the public on topics of general interest.[25]

At the same time, the European Court of Human Rights may exclude the protection of the Convention, in the context of advocacy or incitement to hatred, on the grounds that it is not compatible with the fundamental values of the Convention. Article 10 cannot be invoked to justify hate and regressive speech.[26]

4.1 *Ethnic Hatred*

M'Bala M'Bala v. France[27]

Dieudonné M'Bala M'Bala, a so-called "humorist," was well-known to express extremist political ideas. At the end of one of his shows in Paris in 2008, he invited to the stage Holocaust denier Mr. Faurisson, in order to give him a special award for his insolence and his ability to be hated by everybody. A man, wearing concentration camp clothes and holding a star of David, then proceeded to give him a menorah (a Jewish candelabra) as if it was an Oscar. M'Bala M'Bala was subsequently convicted of public insults against the Jewish people.[28]

M'Bala M'Bala complained about his conviction to the European Court of Human Rights. The Court found he was not entitled to the protection of Article 10, and stressed that his performance was not a show, but a political meeting.

4.1.1 Glorification of Violence or Hatred

Sürek (n°1) v. Turkey[29]

The applicant was the owner of a newspaper magazine that published two letters of readers. Those readers criticized military actions of the authorities in Turkey and accused them of punishing the Kurdish struggle for independence and freedom. The owner of the newspaper was found guilty of an offense of propaganda against the indivisibility of the State and for incitement to hatred.

---

25 *Goodwin v. United Kingdom*, 1996-II Eur.Ct.H.R., App. 17488/90, (1996), http://hudoc.echr.coe.int/eng?i=001-57974.

26 European Convention for the Protection of Human Rights and Fundamental Freedoms, as amended by Protocols Nos. 11 and 14, art. 17, September 3,1953, ETS 5, https://www.coe.int/en/web/conventions/full-list/-/conventions/rms/0900001680063765.

27 *M'Bala M'Bala v. France*, App. 25239/13, Eur.Ct.H.R., November 10, 2015, http://hudoc.echr.coe.int/eng-press?i=003-5219244-6470067.

28 *Id.*

29 *Sürek v. Turkey (No. 1)*, App. 26682/95, 1999-IV Eur.Ct.H.R., http://hudoc.echr.coe.int/eng?i=001-58279.

He argued before the European Court of Human Rights that his freedom of expression had been violated.

The European Court concluded that Article 10 was not violated on the grounds that the letters were inciting hatred and physical violence. According to the Court, the newspaper was used as a tool of dissemination of hate and reinforced this tendency. As the owner of the newspaper, the applicant had special responsibilities, especially in a period of conflicts and war.

4.1.2 Expressing Support for Terrorism

Leroy v. France[30]

The applicant, who was a designer, published in a Basque weekly magazine on September 13, 2001, a symbolic visual picturing the attacks on the World trade center with the following message: "as we had dreamed, Hamas did it." He was convicted of expressing support for terrorism.[31] The applicant argued before the European Court that his conviction violated Article 10 and his freedom of expression. The European Court concluded that there was no violation of his freedom of expression because the drawing glorified violent destruction, expressed moral support to the presumed authors of the world trade center attacks, and was a blow to the human dignity of the victims.

30 *Leroy v. France*, App. 36109/03, Eur.Ct.H.R. http://www.tiesibsargs.lv/files/content/Tiesas_procesa_izspele/Izspelei_noderigi_materiali/ECHR %20Leroy%20v.%20France%2002.10.08_en-1.pdf.

31 *Id.*

Canadian Legal Perspectives on Incitement to Terrorism

Workshop discussions regarding Canadian approaches to incitement to terrorism and hate speech focused on two primary issues: Canadian criminal law before the enactment of Bill C-51,[1] the *Anti-terrorism Act, 2015*,[2] and changes that Bill C-51 introduced.

Before Bill C-51, the Anti-terrorism Act, 2015

In 2001, the Canadian *Criminal Code*[3] was amended by the *Anti-terrorism Act*[4] to create a number of specific terrorism offences. Many of these offences were designed to prevent the carrying out of a terrorist activity. The list of "terrorism offences" enacted at that time included offences such as knowingly participating in or contributing to any activity of a terrorist group for the purpose of enhancing the ability of any terrorist group to facilitate or carry out a terrorist activity, knowingly facilitating a terrorist activity, and committing an indictable offence for the benefit of, at the direction of or in association with a terrorist group.

The maximum punishments for these crimes vary in order to reflect the seriousness of the offence. For example, the maximum punishment for knowingly participating in any activity of a terrorist group, etc. is 10 years imprisonment; the maximum punishment for knowingly facilitating a terrorist activity is 14

* Contributed by a Canadian Justice Department expert. His views do not in any way represent the views of the Department.

1 For the legislative history of Bill C-51, the *Anti-terrorism Act, 2015* which has the full title of *An Act to enact the Security of Canada Information Sharing Act and the Secure Air Travel Act, to amend the Criminal Code, the Canadian Security Intelligence Service Act and the Immigration and Refugee Protection Act and to make related and consequential amendments to other Acts*, *See:* http://www.parl.ca/LegisInfo/BillDetails.aspx?Language=E&billId=6842344.

2 *Anti-terrorism Act, 2015*, S.C. 2015, c.20, http://www.parl.ca/DocumentViewer/en/41-2/bill/C-51/royal-assent.

3 *Criminal Code*, R.S.C., 1985, c. C-46, http://laws-lois.justice.gc.ca/eng/acts/C-46/index.html.

4 *Anti-terrorism Act*, S.C. 2001, c.41, http://www.parl.ca/DocumentViewer/en/37-1/bill/C-36/royal-assent/page-29#3.

 | DOI 10.1163/9789004359826_008

years imprisonment; and the maximum punishment for committing an indictable offence for the benefit of, at the direction of, or in association with a terrorist group is life imprisonment.

In addition, Section 2 of the *Criminal Code* defined "terrorism offence" to mean not only all the above offences, but also conspiracy, attempt, accessory after the fact, or counselling in relation to any of the above offences.[5] The key point is that counselling the commission of a terrorism offence is itself a terrorism offence.

The *Anti-terrorism Act* also defined what is a "terrorist activity." Generally, it is a made-in-Canada definition that has three parts. First, the conduct must be committed for a political, religious or ideological purpose. Second, there must be an intention to intimidate the public with regard to its security or to compel a Government or person to do or refrain from doing something. Third, the person must intentionally cause certain kinds of serious harm, such as causing death or serious bodily harm or causing serious disruption of an essential service or system.[6]

Importantly, the definition of "terrorist activity" also provides that the definition includes a conspiracy, attempt or threat to commit such conduct or being an accessory after the fact or counselling in relation to such a conduct. Note the specific reference to counselling.

So, to summarize, the *Criminal Code* specifically defines counselling the commission of any terrorism offence or any terrorist activity as constituting a terrorism offence or terrorist activity as the case may be.

There are two types of counselling in Canadian criminal law, depending on whether or not the person being counselled to commit a crime did in fact commit the crime. By Subsection 22(1) of the *Criminal Code*, a person who counsels another to commit a crime where that other person commits the crime is a party to the crime and is subject to the same penalty as the person who committed the crime.[7] By Subsection 464(1) of the *Criminal Code*, a person who counsels another to commit a crime where the crime is not committed is also criminally liable.[8] However, the punishment that may be imposed is less than that which would have been imposed had the crime been committed. For example, a person who counsels the commission of murder where the murder is committed must receive a sentence of life imprisonment, but someone who

---

5 *Criminal Code*, R.S.C., 1985, c. C-46, s.2, definition of "terrorism offence," paragraph (d).

6 *Criminal Code*, R.S.C., 1985, c. C-46, s.83.01(1).

7 *Criminal Code*, R.S.C., 1985, c. C-46, s.22(1).

8 *Criminal Code*, R.S.C., 1985, c. C-46, s.464.

counsels another to commit murder where the murder is not committed may receive a maximum punishment of up to 14 years imprisonment.

Now, what does counselling mean? The *Criminal Code*, in Subsection 22(3), defines "counsel" as including procuring, soliciting, or inciting.[9] Thus, incitement is caught by Canadian law under the concept of counselling. However, it has been left to case law to flesh out the *actus reus* and *mens rea* (or mental fault element) for counselling.

The key case in this regard in Canadian criminal law is *R. v. Hamilton*, [2005] 2 S.C.R. 432, a fraud case, decided by the Supreme Court of Canada in 2005. In that case, the Supreme Court ruled that the *actus reus* of counselling is "*the deliberate encouragement or active inducement of the commission of a criminal offence*",[10] or, in other words, active encouragement.

The *mens rea* for counselling is intention or recklessness. As the Supreme Court said: "[T]he *mens rea* consists in nothing less than an accompanying *intent* or *conscious disregard of the substantial and unjustified risk inherent in the counselling*: that is, it must be shown that the accused either intended that the offence counselled be committed, or knowingly counselled the commission of the offence while aware of the unjustified risk that the offence counselled was in fact likely to be committed as a result of the accused's conduct."[11]

There are no specific statutory defences built into the counselling provisions. Nor are there any exemptions to address privacy concerns. Whether the counselling is made in a private conversation between two persons or publicly through the Internet or at a public gathering, the person who counsels the commission of the crime creates an unjustifiable and substantial risk that a crime may be committed and, therefore, faces criminal liability for his or her actions.

So, to summarize so far, in 2001, the *Criminal Code* of Canada created new terrorism offences and a definition of terrorist activity, both of which contained within their definitions the counselling of a terrorism offence or a terrorist activity. More generally, counselling the commission of any crime can lead to criminal liability and punishment whether or not the crime is committed, although if the crime being counselled is not committed a lesser punishment is imposed. Counselling is specifically defined to include incitement. The *actus reus* of counselling is active encouragement and the *mens rea* of counselling is intention or recklessness. Because counselling requires active encouragement, it does not catch instances of glorification of terrorism.

9 Criminal Code, R.S.C., 1985, c. C-46, s.22(3).

10 *R. v. Hamilton*, [2005] 2 S.C.R. 432, 444, para. 29.

11 *Id.*

There is one final point before moving on to the amendments made by Bill C-51, t*he Anti-terrorism Act, 2015*. In 2013, the *Combating Terrorism Act* amended the *Criminal Code* to create four new offences of leaving or attempting to leave Canada in order to commit certain terrorism offences, such as knowingly facilitating a terrorist activity.[12] These are also defined as terrorism offences and so counselling any of these offences would also be defined as a terrorism offence.

After Bill C-51, the Anti-terrorism Act, 2015

It may seem that the counselling or incitement provisions in the *Criminal Code* are comprehensive enough to catch all kinds of active encouragement. However, a person may actively encourage acts of terrorism in general without giving the specific details that would link the encouragement to the commission of a specific terrorism offence.

Consider for a moment the following examples, some of which are hypothetical and some of which are not:

- A DAESH volunteer in Iraq or a sympathizer in Canada using the Internet to call on others to "harm Canadians," without any specificity as to whether the harm encouraged is violence against a person, harm to property or essential services, or providing financial and material support or recruitment to DAESH.
- A DAESH spokesman who reportedly said: "From now on, you have permission to just strike wherever you want ... do whatever is in your capability, just act."
- A DAESH spokesman who said: "O muwahhid, do not let this battle pass you by wherever you may be. You must strike the soldiers, patrons, and troops of the tawāghīt. Strike their police, security, and intelligence members, as well as their treacherous agents. Ruin their sleep. Embitter their lives for them and busy them with themselves."[13]

Would such statements by caught by the regular law of counselling that I have described above? The way that the *Criminal Code* describes the counselling provisions is with reference to counselling a person "to be a party to an offence"

12 *Combating Terrorism Act*, S.C. 2013, c. 9, ss. 6–8.

13 Helen Davidson, *ISIS Instructs Followers to Kill Australians and Other "Disbelievers,"* GUARDIAN, September 23, 2014 (with excerpt from video message).

or "counselling another party to commit an indictable offence," etc. In other words, there is a reference to an offence of some kind to be committed.

There is no problem applying the regular counselling provisions in a situation where it is obvious what crime is being counselled, such as "Kill X" or "Steal from Y" or "Kill X and Steal from Y." The same holds true where someone counsels another to commit a specific terrorism offence, such as where a supporter of DAESH calls upon another to kill someone in order to spread fear among the populace.

The difficulty is that, in the kinds of example described earlier, there is no reference to a specific offence or offences. Hence, it was uncertain whether general statements of the kind made above would in fact be caught by the *Criminal Code*. For, in criminal law, one of the interpretive principles to be applied is the principle that enactments which take away the liberty of the subject should be clear and any ambiguity resolved in favour of the subject.

This could have caused practical and legal impediments to the police and prosecutors if they had wished to prosecute counselling the commission of a terrorism offence where there was no clear factual link to a specific terrorism offence. In such a case, it would have been difficult to say that the person was counselling a specific terrorism offence that could be proven beyond a reasonable doubt.

Furthermore, in such a case, uncertainty would have arisen as to the maximum penalty that could be imposed under the law. Without a specific link to one of the terrorism offences, it followed that there was no specific link to a maximum penalty that could be imposed. Therefore, it would have been difficult to apply the counselling provisions of the *Criminal Code* to determine the appropriate penalty.

Nor would the terrorism offence of instructing the carrying out of a terrorist activity, also found in the *Criminal Code*, be available to prosecute all of these types of examples, because this instructing offence was designed to catch those persons exercising leadership roles, which may not always be the case.[14]

14 *See:* Richard Mosley, "Preventing Terrorism Bill C-36: The *Anti-terrorism Act 2001*" in David Daubney, Wade Deisman et al., editors, *Terrorism, Law and Democracy* (Canadian Institute for the Administration of Justice, 2002), 146, at 165–166. Mr. Mosley, who was at the time the Assistant Deputy Minister, Criminal Law Policy and Community Justice Branch, Department of Justice Canada, explained that the instructing-to-terrorism offences, of which one is the offence set out above, were "leadership" offences that proscribed the serious harm occasioned by those who instruct others to carry out tasks in furtherance of the common objective. He also noted that those caught by the offences may not be at the highest levels of the organization. However, it should be noted that in the case of *R. v. Terezakis*, 2007 BCCA (i.e. British Columbia Court of Appeal) 384, in discussing the

Moreover, because the term "terrorist activity" is narrower in scope than the definition of "terrorism offence" in the *Criminal Code*, the offence of knowingly instructing a terrorist activity is similarly restricted in scope.

For this reason, Bill C-51, the *Anti-terrorism Act, 2015*, created a new offence of advocating or promoting the commission of terrorism offences in general. The offence reads as follows:

> **83.221** (1) Every person who, by communicating statements, knowingly advocates or promotes the commission of terrorism offences in general – other than an offence under this section – while knowing that any of those offences will be committed or being reckless as to whether any of those offences may be committed, as a result of such communication, is guilty of an indictable offence and is liable to imprisonment for a term of not more than five years.[15]

The words "advocates" or "promotes" are used in this offence rather than the word "counselling." While it is true that different words are used, there is no change in meaning from the word "counsels." In *R. v. Keegstra*, [1990] 3 SCR 697, a hate propaganda case, the Supreme Court of Canada said: "the word 'promotes' indicates active support or instigation.... In 'promotes' we thus have a word that indicates more than simple encouragement or advancement."[16] In *R. v. Sharpe*, [2001] 1 SCR 45, a case involving possession of child pornography, the Supreme Court of Canada said: "...in order to meet the requirement of 'advocates' or 'counsels,' the material, viewed objectively, must be seen as 'actively inducing' or encouraging the described offences with children."[17]

The term "terrorism offences in general" refers to the full range of offences as set out in the definition of "terrorism offence" in Section 2 of the *Criminal Code*.

---

constitutionality of the offence of knowingly instructing someone to commit an indictable offence for the benefit of a criminal organization, the Court ruled that there was no need to prove that the person was a leader of the criminal organization, since the crime only requires that a person knowingly instruct that an indictable offence be committed for the benefit of a criminal organization. The Court noted that the ability to give instructions connotes authority, but there was nothing in the language of the offence to require the Crown to prove authority.

15 *Criminal Code*, R.S.C., 1985, c. C-46, s.83.221(1).

16 *R. v. Keegstra* [1990] 3 S.C.R. 697, 776–777, https://scc-csc.lexum.com/scc-csc/scc-csc/en/695/1/document.do.

17 *R. v. Sharpe* [2001] 1 S.C.R. 45, 83, https://scc-csc.lexum.com/scc-csc/scc-csc/en/1837/1/document.do.

The *mens rea* for the offence is meant to mirror the same *mens rea* as for regular counselling, thereby incorporating the concept of recklessness as enunciated by the Supreme Court of Canada in the *Hamilton* case, which was discussed earlier.

There are no statutory defences to this offence, nor is there an exception for private conversations. Again, this is consistent with the regular counselling provisions of the *Criminal Code*.

This offence was designed not to catch instances of glorification of terrorism. This is because the terms "advocates" or "promotes" as defined by the Supreme Court of Canada are restricted to instances of active encouragement. "Glorification" of terrorism lacks this important ingredient of active encouragement, which is why it is sometimes described, as it is in UK law, as a form of indirect encouragement.

To sum up, this new offence was designed to fill what was considered to be a gap in the regular counselling provisions of the *Criminal Code* and was modelled on key elements of the regular counselling regime.

Additional Measures Involving the Offence

Bill C-51 also created new powers for police, when authorized by a court, to seize and forfeit tangible material that constitutes terrorist propaganda or to have terrorist propaganda made available to the public on a computer system to be deleted from the computer system where the computer system is within the jurisdiction the court. "Terrorist propaganda" is defined to mean material that counsels the commission of a terrorism offence or that advocates or promotes the commission of terrorism offences in general.[18] In addition, the *Customs Tariff* was amended to provide customs officers with the authority to prevent the importation of terrorist propaganda, as so defined, into Canada.

Latest Political Developments

The offence of advocating or promoting the commission of terrorism offences in general has been heavily criticized by legal academics and civil liberties organizations in Canada as being an unjustified intrusion on freedom of expression as guaranteed by the *Canadian Charter of Rights and Freedoms*. During

18 *Anti-terrorism Act, 2015*, SC 2015, c. 20, s.16 (adding s.83.222(8) to the Canadian Criminal Code).

the 2015 federal election campaign, the Liberal Party promised to repeal the problematic elements of Bill C-51, and introduce new legislation that better balances the collective security of Canadians with their rights and freedoms. More specifically, they promised to narrow overly broad definitions, such as defining "terrorist propaganda" more clearly. The Liberal Party won a majority in the 2015 election and now forms the Government.

In the fall of 2016, the Government engaged in consultations with Canadians on Canada's national security and the Green Paper that was published to assist the consultation process asked specifically: "Would it be useful to clarify the advocacy offence so that it more clearly resembles counselling?" and "Should the part of the definition of terrorist propaganda referring to the advocacy or promotion of terrorism offences in general be removed from the definition?"[19] The consultation process ended on December 15, 2016.

Subsequently, on June 20, 2017, the Government tabled (at First Reading) Bill C-59, the *National Security Act, 2017*, in the House of Commons of the Canadian Parliament. As of January 2018, Bill C-59 was being considered by a Parliamentary Committee. It proposes to replace the offence of advocating or promoting the commission of terrorism offences in general with a new counselling offence. The proposed new offence reads as follows:

> **Counselling commission of terrorism offence**
> **83.221 (1)** Every person who *counsels another person to commit a* terrorism *offence* – other than an offence under this section – is guilty of an indictable offence and is liable to imprisonment for a term of not more than five years.
>
> **Application**
> **(2)** An offence may be committed under subsection (1) whether or not
> **(a)** a terrorism offence is committed; and
> **(b)** the person counsels the commission of a specific terrorism offence.

As a result, Bill C-59 also proposes to change the definition of terrorist propaganda to mean material that counsels the commission of a terrorism offence. There would no longer be a reference to the offence of "advocating or promoting the commission of terrorism offences in general" in this definition.

The proposed change would make it clearer that what the criminal law should catch is any counselling to commit a terrorism offence, whether or not

19 Government of Canada, *Background Document: Our Security, Our Rights: National Security Green Paper 2016*, https://www.publicsafety.gc.ca/cnt/rsrcs/pblctns/ntnl-scrt-grn-ppr-2016-bckgrndr/ntnl-scrt-grn-ppr-2016-bckgrndr-en.pdf, at 46.

the counselling involves committing a specific terrorism offence. The law governing the *actus reus* and *mens rea* of counselling that is described earlier in this article would be applied to this proposed offence.

The Hate Propaganda Offences in the Canadian Criminal Code

In addition to the various terrorism offences in the *Criminal Code*, since 1970 Canada has three hate propaganda offences, which have expanded in scope over the years by adding to them new groups to be protected. The three offences are:

- advocating or promoting genocide against an identifiable group, found in subsection 318(1) of the *Criminal Code*;
- inciting hatred against an identifiable group by communicating in a public place statements that are likely to lead to a breach of the peace, found in subsection 319(1) of the *Code*; and
- wilfully promoting hatred against an identifiable group other than in private conversation, found in subsection 319(2) of the *Code*.[20]

For the crime of wilfully promoting hatred, there are also defences, such as that the statements were relevant to any subject of public interest, the discussion of which was for the public benefit, and if on reasonable grounds the accused believed them to be true.

"Identifiable group" is defined for these crimes as meaning any section of the public distinguished by colour, race, religion, national or ethnic origin, age, sex, sexual orientation, gender identity or expression, or mental or physical disability.[21]

For the offence of advocating or promoting genocide, the maximum punishment is five years imprisonment; for the other two offences, the maximum punishment is two years imprisonment.

The Supreme Court of Canada held in the case of *R. v. Keegstra*, [1990] 3 SCR 697, that the crime of wilfully promoting hatred against an identifiable group, while violating the freedom of expression guarantee in subsection 2(b) of the *Canadian Charter of Rights of Freedoms*, was nonetheless a justifiable limit on

20 Criminal Code, R.S.C., 1985, c. C-46, s.318(1), 319(1), 319(2).

21 *An Act to Amend the Canadian Human Rights Act and the Criminal Code*, S.C. 2017, C-13, received Royal Assent on June 19, 2017. It added gender identity and gender expression to the definition of "identifiable group" for the hate propaganda offences.

that freedom pursuant to section 1 of the *Charter*.[22] Therefore, it was constitutional. In restricting the scope of the offence, the Supreme Court ruled that the term "promotes" means active support, that the term "hatred" means the most severe form of opprobrium, and that the word "wilfully" means intentionally.[23]

Thus, it may be possible to prosecute someone who incites another person to commit a terrorism offence for a hate propaganda offence as well. This depends on the circumstances of the particular case.

---

22 *R. v. Keegstra* [1990] 3 S.C.R. 697, https://scc-csc.lexum.com/scc-csc/scc-csc/en/695/1/document.do.

23 *R. v. Keegstra* [1990] 3 S.C.R. 697, 773–775, 776–777, 786, https://scc-csc.lexum.com/scc-csc/scc-csc/en/695/1/document.do.

Containing the Proliferation of Incitement: A Canadian Perspective

Christian Leuprecht

During five years living in Kuwait, I was regularly exposed to propaganda about hating Jews, killing Jews, destroying Israel, and killing American co-conspirators. Although I am neither Jewish nor American, this reprehensible discourse shaped my views on incitement, especially for someone of German background.

The prevailing assumption is that the beliefs that people hold are predictive of their behavior; this is the premise on which human security intelligence organizations tend to operate. However, a substantial body of research shows this assumption to be incorrect: many people hold radical views, but few become violent, and not all who become violent had previously been radicalized. People commit extremist violence without necessarily having been radicalized into violent extremism.

A threat has three components: intent, capability, and opportunity. Incitement gives us traction on intent, and when we put that intent in the right context of capability and opportunity, then there is a greater probability of people moving from thought to action. Incitement, then, is a catalyst. As such, it then raises a comparative problem. If violence were driven by incitement and the internet, then we would expect to find roughly the same phenomenon with roughly similar traction across different countries. But that is not the case. Incitement is far more prolific in some countries than in others. So is violence: some countries struggle more with violence than others. This suggests that there are endogenous effects at work.

Incitement does not seem to fit neatly into any of the categories we commonly use: it is not terrorism *per se*, it is not like terrorism, but it is also not hate speech. Pre-emptive responses can be divided into three: criminal, administrative and investigative. There is some activity that societies have long decided to designate as terrorism – politically-motivated violent extremism is terrorism. Then there are activities that are not terrorism *per se*, but that society has deemed to be akin to terrorism, such as financing or procurement to enable terrorism. These activities are the focus of prosecutors and their responses are commonly referred to as criminal preemption. Beyond that are measures of administrative preemption: confiscating passports or making it

 | DOI 10.1163/9789004359826_009

more difficult for people to travel and spread propaganda. Investigative preemption is akin to the Al Capone approach: if a perpetrator proves difficult to charge with terrorism, then take that individual out of circulation on a different infraction, such as tax evasion.

Much of the legislative and operational innovation is being driven in these three domains: criminal, administrative, and investigative preemption. In my view, better prevention of incitement requires improving the tools that are at our disposal in the legal context.

Legal tools for addressing "incitement to hate" focus on defining the threshold for criminal extremism, such as terrorism or actions equated with terrorism. But terrorism investigations are cumbersome, and the standard of evidence for conviction high. That means relatively few investigations that consume a disproportionate amount of resources. With law enforcement resources constrained by fiscal austerity, criminal prosecution is unlikely to prove an effective strategy at reining in the inflationary growth of incitement. An alternative strategy is to harness opportunities for confronting incitement in the pre-criminal space.

The challenges of incitement and Internet pornography are quite similar. Pornography used to be about "soft" porn; the hard-core remained largely out of sight. As a result of the media, hard-core porn has gone mainstream, and is on the verge of being a public health epidemic. Similarly, offensive hate discourse used to be quite marginal, and restricted to small communities of sympathizers. The Internet has enabled incitement to go mainstream: it is anonymous, inexpensive, and proliferates. Youth are required to hold licenses to drive cars; but children have virtually unrestricted access to the most demeaning forms of pornography – and incitement. In the same way that pornography verges on a public health crisis, incitement verges on a national security crisis. The extent of this crisis necessitates a broader discussion about solutions.

The ability to restrict and prosecute certain types of speech is one of the main differences between the United States and other democracies. The difference becomes evident when one compares constitutional provisions that protect freedom of speech in the United States with those in Canada that protect freedom of expression.[1] In general, in the United States it has proven virtually impossible to restrict speech of just about any kind. By contrast, the rest of the democratic world, including Canada, has long had a broad

1 Canadian Charter of Rights and Freedoms, s.2(b). Enacted as Schedule B to the Canada Act 1982, 1982, c. 11 (U.K.), which came into force on April 17, 1982.

democratic consensus that not all forms of speech warrant equal protection. Rather, speech has to be meaningful, and make a positive contribution to society. The democratic social contract outside of the United States holds that inciting hate is unacceptable in general, and in particular, inciting hate against any identifiable group violates the protection of minority rights deemed essential for a vibrant, pluralistic, and tolerant civil society and democratic culture.

The Criminal Code of Canada has for many years had provisions against hate speech and hate crimes.[2] There is also a sentencing provision that encourages judges to consider whether a crime was motivated by hate.[3] Judges have greater latitude at the sentencing stage to consider more severe penalties in cases where the crime was motivated by hate.

The burden of proof to convict someone of hate is quite stringent.[4] The speech must be the most severe of the genre. The hate must target an identifiable group. It must be public. It must be deliberate and not careless. Excluded from hate speech are good faith interpretations of religious doctrine, discussion of issues of public interest, and literary devices such as sarcasm and irony. The statements must be hateful when considered in a social and historical context. And no prosecution can proceed without approval of the Attorney General, which introduces political accountability because the Attorney General is also a Cabinet Minister.

The Supreme Court of Canada has added an additional layer over and above these particular provisions: the Canadian Constitution protects not only free

2 Sections 318, 319, and 329 of the Criminal Code of Canada criminalize the use of hate propaganda (advocating or promoting genocide) and public incitement to hatred in Canada.

3 Criminal Code of Canada, s.718.2 ("a court that imposes a sentence shall also take into consideration the following principles: (a) a sentence should be increased or reduced to account for any relevant aggravating or mitigating circumstance relating to the offence or the offender, and, without limiting the generality of the foregoing, (i) evidence that the offence was motivated by bias, prejudice or hate based on race, national or ethnic origin, language, colour, religion, sex, age, mental, or physical disability, sexual orientation, or any other similar factor…").

4 Criminal Code of Canada, s.319(1) outlines that everyone who, by communicating statements in any public place, incites hatred against any identifiable group where such incitement is likely to lead to a breach of the peace is guilty of (a) an indictable offence and is liable to imprisonment for a term not exceeding two years; or (b) an offence punishable on summary conviction. Section 319(2) mandates that everyone who, by communicating statements, other than in private conversation, willfully promotes hatred against any identifiable group is guilty of (a) an indictable offence and is liable to imprisonment for a term not exceeding two years; or (b) an offence punishable on summary conviction. Section 319(3) lists four circumstances where a person shall not be convicted of an offence under Subsection 319(2).

expression, but multiculturalism and equality as well.[5] Ergo, the Constitution cannot permit one protected freedom to undermine other rights and freedoms that enjoy equal status. The Supreme Court of Canada has also recognized the insidious impact of propaganda campaigns that gain social traction in incrementally dull rational faculties and empathy.[6] Broadly, then, there is recognition that speech that falls into this category is not socially productive or desirable. The Courts have held that even if a hate speech prohibition has never been used, it has symbolic value. The main purpose of the Canadian Criminal Code provisions is not necessarily to prosecute, but to deter and to set clear standards for expected discourse. The Canadian Supreme Court agrees that hate speech has no redeeming value.[7]

This stands in stark contrast to the United States. In the U.S., speech protections are old laws and old provisions. Crafted at a time when absolute monarchs sought to stifle dissent, the aim was to emphasize that freedom of speech is integral to democracy. In contrast, in Canada and much of the rest of the world, free expression norms are reactions to the Holocaust. They developed in the second half of the 20th century in recognition that nothing of the sort must happen again, and that incitement was a major catalyst for the Holocaust and related events.

Incitement goes beyond intimidating, harming, or terrifying one particular person. Rather, it is directed at an entire group of people to which the victim belongs and with which the victim identifies (or is identified). That is, victims are not targeted for who they are or for what they have done. This approach is embedded in the Canadian ethic of multicultural accommodation and respect. A diverse set of cases has been prosecuted under these provisions: Holocaust deniers and people looking to spread related propaganda,[8] a cross burning in

5 Canadian Charter of Rights and Freedoms, s.15(1), 27. Enacted as Schedule B to the Canada Act 1982, 1982, c. 11 (U.K.), which came into force on April 17, 1982 ("Every individual is equal before and under the law and has the right to the equal protection and equal benefit of the law without discrimination and, in particular, without discrimination based on race, national or ethnic origin, colour, religion, sex, age or mental or physical disability.") *Id.* at s.27: This Charter shall be interpreted in a manner consistent with the preservation and enhancement of the multicultural heritage of Canadians.

6 David Butt, *Canada's Law on Hate Speech is embodiment of compromise*, THE GLOBE AND MAIL, January 19, 2015, http://www.theglobeandmail.com/opinion/canadas-law-on-hate-speech-is-the-embodiment-of-compromise/article22520419/.

7 *Saskatchewan Human Rights Commission v. Whatcott*, 2013 S.C.C. 11, ¶171.

8 *See for example*: *Zundel* (*Re*), 2005 FC 295, [2005], F.C.J. No. 314 (QL), ¶¶16, 17 (upholding the inadmissibility determination regarding Ernst Zündel, a permanent resident of Canada, on

New Brunswick on the front lawn of a home of a multi-racial family,[9] a child seized by Child Protective Services in Manitoba whom the stepfather sent to school wearing a Swastika and Nazi symbols (the Courts agreed that this child should not be returned to the stepfather.)[10] In other words, these provisions and their enforcement are fairly robust.

Canada does not guarantee freedom of speech in the Canadian Charter of Rights and Freedoms: it guarantees freedom of expression. In the words of the Charter: "2. Everyone has the following fundamental freedoms: ...(b) freedom of thought, belief, opinion and expression..."[11] The term imposes certain limits, which is why the Canadian Supreme Court has decided that there are no redeemable qualities to hate speech.

At the same time, the freedom is subject to a general clause qualifying all of the Charter's rights and freedoms: "Section 1: The Canadian Charter of Rights and Freedoms guarantees the rights and freedoms set out in it subject only to such reasonable limits prescribed by law as can be demonstrably justified in a free and democratic society."[12] The reasonable limits test allows the government to pass legislation that infringes rights and freedoms that are protected in the Charter, provided that the legislation, its intent, and how it is framed and phrased, passes certain benchmarks that have been articulated by the Supreme Court. The Charter also contains a so-called "notwithstanding clause" that would allow Parliament to override some provisions that might be nullified by the Court, but this clause has fallen into disuse.[13] However, the existence of the clause does set up a dialog between Parliament and the Courts, rather than the more black-and-white approach to such issues in the United States. The combination of the reasonable limits clause and the notwithstanding clause have thus informed how Canada interprets and applies counterterrorism provisions.

---

grounds of security, specifically based on evidence that Mr. Zündel associated, supported and directed members of the White Supremacist Movement who in one fashion or another sought to propagate violent messages of hate and have advocated the destruction of governments and multicultural societies).

9 *R. v. Rehberg*, 2010 NSPC 101.

10 *Director of Child and Family Services v. D.M.P. et al.*, 2010 MBQB 32.

11 Canadian Charter of Rights and Freedoms, s.2(b). Enacted as Schedule B to the Canada Act 1982, 1982, c. 11 (U.K.), which came into force on April 17, 1982.

12 Canadian Charter of Rights and Freedoms, s.1. Enacted as Schedule B to the Canada Act 1982, 1982, c. 11 (U.K.), which came into force on April 17, 1982.

13 Canadian Charter of Rights and Freedoms, s.33. Enacted as Schedule B to the Canada Act 1982, 1982, c. 11 (U.K.), which came into force on April 17, 1982.

Canada adopted significant changes to its counter-terrorism law in 2015. Bill C-51[14] was partially meant to close a loophole with regards to facilitation of terrorism. The concern was that "freedom of expression" could be used to evade a charge of facilitation. The government felt that it was important to clarify that no one should be allowed to communicate knowingly for the purpose of actively inducing the commission of a terrorist offense.[15] The focus was on intent, not glorification. The possession of material, in and of itself, is not an offence. Using that material to counsel is. That is the deterrent effect the legislation is meant to achieve.

The incitement provision in current Canadian legislation works because it is couched in the context of a number of other provisions. For instance, the government extended the possible length of "peace bonds."[16] Instead of immediately having to arrest and charge a suspect, the government can have a judge impose an authorization in the form of a "peace bond," wherein the suspect agrees not to engage in certain types of activity. The prohibition may include agreement not to wander further than a certain distance from one's home, not to drive a car, or not to access the internet. The process affords authorities some latitude to contain a risk. There are Canadians who are currently subject to peace bonds as a result of the incitement provision; the individuals have agreed to refrain from certain activity in return for not being charged.

These provisions are also applicable to recognizance: a suspect can be kept in initial detention for a longer period of time under the provisions of C-51.[17]

---

14 Bill C-51: *An Act to enact the Security of Canada Information Sharing Act and the Secure Air Travel Act, to amend the Criminal Code, the Canadian Security Intelligence Service Act and the Immigration and Refugee Protection Act and to make related and consequential amendments to other Acts*, (2015) Royal Assent June 18, 2015, 41st Parliament, 2nd Session., http://www.parl.gc.ca/HousePublications/Publication.aspx?Language=E&Mode=1&DocId=8056977.

15 Tonda MacCharles *Conservative ministers downplay concerns about terror bill*, TORONTO STAR, March 10, 2015, https://www.thestar.com/news/canada/2015/03/10/conservative-ministers-downplay-concerns-terror-bill-infringes-on-freedoms.html.

16 Bill C-51: An Act to enact the Security of Canada Information Sharing Act and the Secure Air Travel Act, to amend the Criminal Code, the Canadian Security Intelligence Service Act and the Immigration and Refugee Protection Act and to make related and consequential amendments to other Acts, (2015) Royal Assent June 18, 2015, 41st Parliament, 2nd Session., http://www.parl.gc.ca/HousePublications/Publication.aspx?Language=E&Mode=1&DocId=8056977, s.8.1 (states that if the judge is also satisfied that the person was convicted previously of a terrorism offence, the judge may order that the person enter into the recognizance for a period of not more than two years).

17 Bill C-51, Section 15 (5) amends the Criminal Code of Canada by extending the period under which a person may be ordered into recognizance to two years.

These changes also provide what is now known as the threat mitigation or diminishment mandate for the Canadian Security Intelligence Service (CSIS). Technically speaking, for example, CSIS did not previously have the powers to talk to parents or seek out parents whose children might be either viewing incitement material or engaging in conversations or communications involving incitement. C-51 now explicitly allows CSIS to disrupt this type of activity by allowing CSIS to engage with families and with communities, some of whose members may be subject to or engaged in incitement.[18] In addition, the evidentiary threshold for CSIS to conduct surveillance is lower.[19] In return, the intelligence CSIS gathers can, by and large, not be introduced in court for the purpose of criminal prosecution.

Bill C-51 also allows authorities to apply to remove material from the Internet – provided the services that provide the material are in Canada.[20]

18 Bill C-51: An Act to enact the Security of Canada Information Sharing Act and the Secure Air Travel Act, to amend the Criminal Code, the Canadian Security Intelligence Service Act and the Immigration and Refugee Protection Act and to make related and consequential amendments to other Acts, (2015) Royal Assent June 18, 2015, 41st Parliament, 2nd Session., http://www.parl.gc.ca/HousePublications/Publication.aspx?Language=E&Mode=1&DocId=8056977, s.42 (1) (amends the CSIS Act by adding the following after Section 12: "if there are reasonable grounds to believe that a particular activity constitutes a threat to the security of Canada, the Service may take measures, within or outside Canada, to reduce that threat").

19 Bill C-51: An Act to enact the Security of Canada Information Sharing Act and the Secure Air Travel Act, to amend the Criminal Code, the Canadian Security Intelligence Service Act and the Immigration and Refugee Protection Act and to make related and consequential amendments to other Acts, (2015) Royal Assent June 18, 2015, 41st Parliament, 2nd Session., http://www.parl.gc.ca/HousePublications/Publication.aspx?Language=E&Mode=1&DocId=8056977, s.17.1, (amended paragraphs 83.3(2)(a) and (b) of the Criminal Code to allow peace officers, to subject to Subsection (1), to lay information before a provincial court judge if the peace officer (a) believes on reasonable grounds that a terrorist activity *may be carried out* [emphasis added]; and (b) suspects on reasonable grounds that the imposition of a recognizance with conditions on a person, or the arrest of a person, is likely to prevent the carrying out of the terrorist activity. Previously, Section 83.3 (2) of the Criminal Code stated that subject to Subsection (1), a peace officer may lay an information before a provincial court judge if the peace officer (a) believes on reasonable grounds that a terrorist activity will be carried out; and (b) suspects on reasonable grounds that the imposition of a recognizance with conditions on a person, or the arrest of a person, is necessary to prevent the carrying out of the terrorist activity.).

20 Criminal Code of Canada, s.83.223(1) (states that if a judge is satisfied by information on oath that there are reasonable grounds to believe that there is material – that is terrorist propaganda or computer data that makes terrorist propaganda available – stored on and made available to the public through a computer system that is within the court's

When particular thresholds are met, departments may share data for particular purposes on those individuals. This facilitates inter-agency coordination and a more concerted approach to threats, including incitement.

Some of the consequences of Bill C-51 are as yet unknown. One of the challenges facing prosecutors is a high evidentiary threshold. Crown Prosecutors are also apprehensive about prosecuting incitement because to-date there is little precedent or case law.[21] Moreover, the Bill, adopted by Canada's Conservative government in March 2015, has been undergoing a review by a Liberal government elected thereafter.[22]

Other recent legal developments in Canada to tackle incitement include extraterritorial prosecutions that extend the reach of Canadian law beyond Canada's boundaries to hold Canadians to account for actions abroad, and to hold foreigners to account for targeting Canadians. States need to be enabled to prosecute their own citizens and legal residents who travel abroad for purposes that include incitement. Authorities also need to improve operationally their ability to carry out sensitive investigations. Few countries are actually able to conduct extraterritorial prosecutions because they are legally and operationally very complex. Nonetheless, prosecution should also be seen as only one approach among multiple options that authorities have at their disposal.

Incitement is not black and white and has many nuances. In Canada, the perpetrator of the Orlando shooting[23] would have likely ended up subject to a peace bond that probably would have thwarted the attack. In the end, the

jurisdiction, the judge may order the computer system's custodian to (a) give an electronic copy of the material to the court (b) ensure that the material is no longer stored on and made available through the computer system; and (c) provide the information that is necessary to identify and locate the person who posted the material).

21 Farah Mohamed Shirdon was charged in absentia with utterance or threats towards Canada and the United States in September 2015. Stewart Bell, *Calgary man who joined ISIL charged with terrorism, "utterance of threats towards Canada,"* National Post, September 24, 2015, http://news.nationalpost.com/news/canada/calgary-man-who-joined-isil-charged-with-terrorism-utterance-of-threats-towards-canada.

22 The Liberal government launched a public online consultation in September 2016 to get feedback on Canada's national security laws and policies. The consultation ended in December 2016. In February 2017, the government announced that information gathered from this public consultation was being compiled and a report on the findings will be made to the public in 2017. *Consultation on National Security*, Government of Canada, https://www.canada.ca/en/services/defence/nationalsecurity/consultation-national-security.html (last accessed July 11, 2017).

23 *Orlando Shooting*, New York Times, https://www.nytimes.com/news-event/2016-orlando-shooting (last accessed July 11, 2017).

state needs a toolkit that is broader than simply prosecution to contain the proliferation of incitement.

Incitement is like learning a language. Travelling to a new country and trying to communicate, one needs to acquire and familiarize oneself with the local vernacular. That includes learning to operationalize the language within its context. Incitement encourages people to acquire an understanding of a particular linguistic tool and to provide a context for that tool that may influence a person's behavior. It needs to be more difficult for people to be exposed to the socialization and the learning mechanisms associated with incitement. Ultimately, our objective should be restricting access to incitement as an accelerant that fuels the fire.

Incitement and Related Matters in Israeli Law

The workshop discussions on incitement, and matters related to incitement, in Israeli law focused on eight primary points.

1. In 2016, after years of terrorist attacks, the Knesset enacted a law dealing specifically with terror – the Struggle Against Terror Law, 2016.[1] The Law deals with many aspects of terror and it gives the State a wide range of legal means with which to fight terrorism. It grants ministers the authority to declare various bodies as "Terrorist Organizations," and it gives authority to seize, confiscate and manage property of a "Terrorist Organization."

   In addition, it establishes a long list of offences relating to different aspects of terrorism. The offences include special offences dealing with incitement to terrorism. Up to the enactment of the Law in 2016 one could find criminal offences relating to terrorism in various enactments, some of them go back to the time of the British Mandate. Some of these provisions were abolished by the new law.
2. When dealing with the subject of incitement in Israeli Law, one should mention also provisions in laws that relate to political parties and to elections, both national and local.

   In these laws one finds provisions that deal with incitement and related matters. Thus in the Parties Law, 1992 there is a section that says that a party with certain purposes or that committed specific deeds cannot be registered with the Parties Registrar.

   The forbidden purposes or actions are –
   a. Negation of the existence of Israel as a Jewish and democratic state;
   b. Incitement to racism;
   c. Support of armed struggle against the State of Israel by a hostile state or a terrorist organization;
   d. Reasonable basis for the conclusion that the party would serve as a cover to illegal activities.[2]

---

* Not all expert participants in the December 9, 2016 workshop contributed on the record.

1 Combatting Terrorism Law 5776–2016, http://fs.knesset.gov.il//20/law/20_lsr_343902.pdf (in Hebrew).

2 Parties Law, 5752–1992, s.5.

 | DOI 10.1163/9789004359826_010

The first three (a, b and c) also appear in Basic Law: The Knesset, when the Law specifies what lists and what candidates cannot participate in Knesset elections.[3] In other words, a list or a candidate will not be approved to run for elections to the Knesset if one of their purposes is denial of Israel as a Jewish and democratic state, incitement to racism or support of armed struggle against Israel. A somewhat similar provision appears in the law that regulates municipal elections. One can find such provisions also in other laws, for example those that regulate election advertising and advertising on television and radio.

3. The various provisions about incitement and related issues raise difficult questions about their constitutionality and interpretation. The section in Basic Law: The Knesset about purposes of lists and candidates also brings to the fore questions about the right to be elected in a democracy.

The Israeli Supreme Court has been wrestling with the dilemmas for decades.

Although the issue was not discussed in detail with respect to freedom of speech but rather from the aspect of the right to be elected and the right to vote, the matter is closely related. The issue reached the Court in 1965, before Basic Law: The Knesset included a specific provision that authorized the Central Election Committee not to approve lists that wanted to run in Knesset Elections because of the purposes or the actions of the lists.[4] In that case, a list that was not approved by the Committee petitioned the Court against the decision of the Committee not to approve it because the people who formed the list were against the very existence of the State of Israel.

The Supreme Court held (by a four to one majority) that the Committee had that authority even though there was nothing in the Basic Law (or in any other law) dealing specifically with this matter. The Court based its conclusion on the basic right of every democratic country to defend itself against those who seek its destruction.

4. In 1985, a new section was added to Basic Law: The Knesset and it gave the Central Elections Committee specific power not to approve a list of candidates that wished to run in Knesset elections.[5] At that time the authority of the Committee covered situations where the purposes or

---

3 Basic Law: The Knesset (5718–1958), s.7a(a), http://knesset.gov.il/laws/special/eng/BasicLawTheKnesset.pdf.

4 EA 1/65 *Yardor v. Chairman of the Central Elections Committee*, 19 P.D (3) 365 (in Hebrew).

5 Basic Law: The Knesset (5718–1958), s.7a, http://knesset.gov.il/laws/special/eng/BasicLawTheKnesset.pdf.

actions of the list negated the existence of the State of Israel as the country of the Jewish people, negated the democratic character of the State, or incited to racism. The section was amended a few times and now, as mentioned before, it covers negation of the existence of the State as Jewish and democratic, incitement to racism and support of armed struggle against the State of Israel by an enemy state or a terrorist organization. The Court had to grapple with the interpretation of the section when both Jewish and Arab lists with extreme agendas wished to face the electorate in Knesset elections. The Supreme Court said more than once that only in very special and rare cases it would be justified not to approve a list or a candidate.[6] The Court was acutely aware that one of the basic tenets of a democracy is the right of every citizen to associate with others and to run in general elections. In fact, in most cases brought before the Court it decided that the list or the specific candidate can run in the coming elections.

5. The new Israeli law that deals with the fight against terrorism is very comprehensive. In addition to criminal offences it grants various governmental bodies wide powers to fight terrorism. Now mention will be made of the criminal offences that cover incitement and related matters. The relevant section in the law, Section 24, establishes several offences and mentions, among others, publishing in public words of support of a terrorist organization and direct call for the commission of a terrorist act.[7] At the same time, it specifically excludes a true and fair report about a forbidden publication.

6. How will the courts of Israel handle prosecutions under Section 24 of the new law? It is almost obvious that the courts will have to deal with constitutional challenges and issues of interpretation. The constitutional argument will be that Section 24, or at least some of the offences therein, are inconsistent with freedom of speech.[8] Though this freedom is not specifically mentioned in Basic Law: Human Dignity and Liberty,[9] it can be claimed that freedom of speech is a derivative of human dignity and therefore protected by the Basic Law. The constitutional question would be affected by the way the courts of Israel would interpret the various

6 *See for example:* EA 23/84 *Neiman v. Central Election Committee*, 39(2) PD 225 (in Hebrew).

7 Combatting Terrorism Law (5776–2016), s.24, http://fs.knesset.gov.il//20/law/20_lsr_343902.pdf (in Hebrew).

8 Compare this with *Holder v. Humanitarian Law Project*, 561 U.S 1 (2010).

9 Basic Law: Human Dignity and Liberty (5752–1992), http://knesset.gov.il/laws/special/eng/BasicLawLiberty.pdf.

offences. A narrow interpretation may help deflect the constitutional challenge. It should be noted that the Basic Law: Human Dignity and Liberty contains a grandfather clause that immunizes old laws from a constitutional challenge. Thus, when the Law of 2016 was enacted and abolished some old provisions, it opened the way to constitutional challenges that could not be directed against the old laws.

In terms of interpretation, the courts will have to decide which of the new offences are only behavioral and which are consequential, that is, which offences include only elements of behavior and which ones are more limited. In order to convict, the prosecution must prove, in addition to the proscribed behavior, that in consequence it is near certain, probable or possible and maybe imminent (again a matter of interpretation) that the harm would materialize.

7. The Israeli courts will have to face, like courts in other countries, the issue of incitement on the Internet and social media. The new technology with its great advantages in wider access by the common person to the elites and to political decision-makers poses, at the same time, some problems. The new media is typified by anonymity, direct communication (without intermediaries), absence of national boundaries and low cost. These characteristics present new challenges to the legislatures and the courts in democratic countries. The fact that an inciting post or a vitriolic blog can reach millions of people in seconds even on the other side of the globe makes it very difficult for the authorities of one country to regulate and address challenges. There is a need for international cooperation not only between governments but also between governments and the companies that operate the social media.

In May 2016, the European Commission reached an agreement with Facebook, Twitter and YouTube.[10] The purpose of the agreement is to combat the spread of illegal hate speech online. The companies undertook to address complaints and to remove hate speech within twenty-four hours of receipt of notification. Obviously, there will be debates whether a specific item crossed the line. The question is who will be the final arbiter. Even if the item is removed within twenty-four hours, in some cases it may be too late. Still, this agreement moves in the right direction.

8. To sum up: Israeli law deals with various aspects of incitement, including incitement to terrorism through criminal offences and limits on the right

10 *See*: *European Commission and IT Companies announce Code of Conduct on illegal online hate speech*, European Commission, May 31, 2016, http://europa.eu/rapid/press-release_IP-16-1937_en.htm.

to be elected. At the same time, the Israeli Supreme Court interpreted the provisions that allow the Central Elections Committee to block lists and candidates from running in election in such a way that in practice that power could be legally used only in very rare and extreme cases. One can expect a similar approach when the Israeli courts will have to decide cases involving the offences in the Struggle Against Terror Law, 2016, that criminalize different aspects of incitement.

Fighting Incitement: The Work and Practice of the Israeli Prosecution 2014–2016

Erez Padan

Since 2014, the phenomenon of incitement to violence and terror on racial and security grounds in Israel has been taking on greater dimensions. Most of the growth is related to the platform of social networks and the virtual space. These have added to forms of "traditional" incitement in speeches, articles, pamphlets etc. Evidence regarding the influence of incitement, not merely on the views and conceptions of audiences, but on individuals taking part in murderous terrorist attacks, is available to us through the statements of the perpetrators in their interrogations. From a law enforcement perspective, these developments have created significant challenges. In our following notes, we will address some the major issues in the practice of the prosecution in Israel fighting incitement offenses in light of this new reality.

In the summer of 2014, following a number of incidents – the kidnapping and murder of three Jewish boys, the kidnapping and murder of an Arab boy, and "Operation Protective Edge" – we learned that the dimensions and implications of incitement to terror and violence have intensified; it seemed that inciting racist or violent statements, including calls to harm the innocent, were being distributed at a higher frequency and intensity than before.

The State of Israel, as a democratic state, is committed to freedom of expression as a fundamental right, which also includes the right to publish extreme harsh and even galling statements and infuriating opinions the majority of the public detests. However, this right is not unlimited, and there are various offenses in criminal law limiting the right and restricting it. The main legal provisions are sections 144A, 144D2 of the Penal Law.[1] Section 144A prescribes a penalty of five years imprisonment for publication with the aim of incitement to racism. Section 144D2 of the Penal Law prohibits a call to commit an act of violence or terrorism, and also the publication of words of praise, sympathy

---

* This chapter is based on a paper prepared at the Israel Ministry of Justice, State Attorney Office and other material collected by the author at the Jerusalem District Attorney Office.

1 Israel Penal Law (5737–1977), https://www.nevo.co.il/law_html/Law01/073_002.htm (in Hebrew).

 | DOI 10.1163/9789004359826_011

or encouragement of an act of violence or terrorism, if as a result of the inciting publication's content and the circumstances under which it was published, there is a tangible possibility that it will lead to committing an act of violence or terrorism. The penalty prescribed alongside this offense is up to five years imprisonment. Recently a new anti-terror law was enacted,[2] introducing a new offense – Section 24 entitled: "Demonstrating Sympathy for A Terror Organization and Incitement to terrorism." In order to convict in an offense of a call to commit an act of terrorism, no proof of a tangible possibility that the call will lead to the committing of an act of terrorism is required as was previously the case, and the very fact of the call should be sufficient in order to enable prosecution. The penalty prescribed for this offense is either two, three or five years imprisonment according to the three levels of severity designated in the subsections of this offense.[3]

---

2 Combatting Terrorism Law 5776–2016, s.24, http://fs.knesset.gov.il//20/law/20_lsr_343902.pdf (in Hebrew).

3 An example of an indictment issued during 2016, that involved publications on Facebook, is the case of State of Israel v. Samer Rajabi, Jerusalem Magistrate's Court) 11220-01-16, (2016). Entries from the Facebook page of Samer Rajabi included the following instances of incitement to commit an act of violence or terrorism: (1) November 20, 2011, an image of a knife-wielding man slashing a person who is on the ground, with blood spattering, and an image of the Dome of the Rock in the background. The image is accompanied by the words "Jerusalem is shedding tears and El-Aqsa is imprisoned, I wish I could wipe your tears and break you loose. I don't know why our city is in sorrow and mourning as the land continues to soak the blood of our young … we have swore [sic] to god we will protect you and sacrifice our soul for you. Farewell the nation of shame … Jerusalem is for us and no one will enter El-Aqsa but our honorable … this is our promise … the one god is the shaheed." (2) July 29, 2014, an image of an individual carrying a gun. The image is accompanied by the words "Shock them Kasam," "Battalions of Az Adin El Kasam." (This is the military unit of Hamas). (3) October 3, 2014, an image of fighters in masks with guns. The image is accompanied by the words "Gaza will rebel in face of pain." (4) November 21, 2014, images of a hand that is holding a molotov cocktail and individuals with victory signs in the air in front of flames rising from the ground. It is accompanied by the words "Death to Israel" (in Hebrew and Arabic) "Little Gaza #Silwan. (5) February 14, 2015, an image of the face of two men. It is accompanied by the words "May God have mercy for you in heaven" and "A crazy is he who still has fear in his Heart for Al-Aqsa mosque when there are such men in his land." (The men in the picture murdered six worshipers and injured seven in a terror attack in a synagogue in Har-Nof, Jerusalem in November 2014). (6) May 4, 2015, images of mean in combat gear surrounding a small girl also dressed in combat gear who is also carrying a rifle. It is accompanied by the words "Say hello. A Palestinian girl is in front of you." (7) May 6, 2015, images of two men in combat gear holding weapons and between them a very small child also dressed in combat

Utilizing these legal tools, indictments are filed against inciters in cases where a sufficient evidentiary foundation has been established, and when the prosecution finds that filing charges is in the public's interest, after obtaining the approval of the Attorney General.

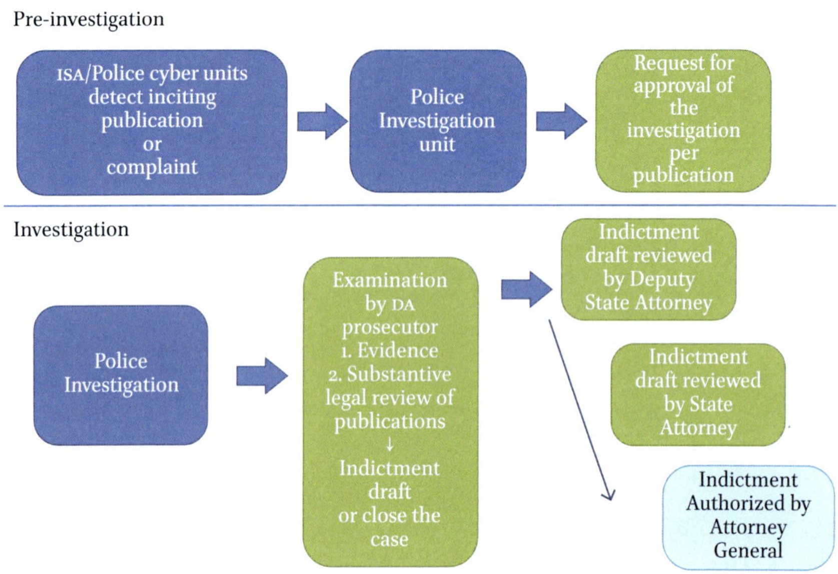

FIGURE 1 *Flow chart – the work process on incitement cases*

---

gear. It is accompanied by the words "My child, study your Topography. Either I will go back with you, or you will walk alone. Our way if victory of Martyrdom." (8) October 4, 2015, an image of Mohammed Jaabis slumped dead in a tractor. It is accompanied with the words "The anniversary of the hero martyr Muhammed Jaabis who killed one Settler and injured five." (Moments before he was shot by police at the scene, Jaabis had used a tractor to ram into a bus, running over and killing one man and wounding others.) (9) October 12, 2015, an image of a facebook "like" hand holding a knife. (On October 12, 2016 there were 4 terror attacks with knives in Jerusalem on the same day. Two citizens were badly wounded.) Entries from the Facebook page of Samer Rajabi also included instances demonstrating sympathy for a terror organization: (1) April 22, 2015, an image of a logo with an inscription that reads "Al Kutla al Islamia our choice" and "Congratulations to Hamas for the victory over Fatah youth." (Al Kutla al Islamia is the students branch of Hamas) (2) November 14, 2015, an image of a man. It is accompanied by the words "You were the teacher and the leader and the martyr. You have always been the courageous lion, you still live in our hearts and Palestine will not forget you. With God's help, you will reach heaven." The man is Ahamad Jaabari, former leader of Hamas' military wing.

It should be noted that the enforcement actions carried out in respect of the incitement to violence phenomenon are, without exception, independent of the nationality or origin of the suspect, and regardless of the political affiliation of the defendant or the complainant. In all cases, the examination of the facts is carried out on a professional and pertinent basis only.

From 2014 until today, the prosecution has submitted over 70 indictments for incitement to violence, terrorism and racism. In most cases, the defendants were prosecuted for posting on their Facebook account praise or direct calls for violence and terror against civilians and the security forces, as well as words of support of a terrorist organization. A large portion of the defendants have no previous criminal record, and a significant number of the defendants are minors.

As part of the response to the rising incitement, in most cases, the police investigation includes pre-trial detention. If the case goes to trial, then the prosecution files alongside with the indictment a request for detention of the defendant until the end of the proceedings. In many cases, the request is granted, including when the defendant is a minor. One of the reasons for this strict law enforcement is the evidence available to us today regarding the influence of incitement on individuals that have committed or attempted terror attacks. The most recent wave of violence starting September 2015 was led by youths, mainly teenagers, boys and girls who acted independently of any terrorist cell or organization. In their interrogations, some have made it clear that they were influenced by the incitement on the media either on television or social media. One illuminating example was a statement by a 15-year-old Palestinian girl who attempted to murder a Jew in the old city of Jerusalem with a knife (luckily she was spotted stalking the victim and arrested beforehand). In her interrogation, relating to questions about her motives, she said that she had been frequently watching the El-Aktza TV channel, and stated that "even if you don't think of stabbing, you watch El-Aktza and you feel you have to do this." In young terrorists' cases, it is not unusual to hear the defense attorneys arguing for a softer sentence, because the defendant was pushed to action by incitement. It seems that today more than ever before, we can attach specific terror crimes to incitement, not only as a common sense conclusion, but on grounds of statements of the perpetrators.

Another aspect of the prosecution's policy change and the desire to take a hard line with defendants convicted of incitement is the work towards raising the punitive bar towards significant imprisonment time. In most cases, the prosecution's motions are granted and defendants convicted are sent to carry out sentences ranging from 8 to 14 months in prison. For example, the Jerusalem Magistrates Court recently sentenced the defendant Khalid Mughrabi to

11 months imprisonment and a 6 month suspended sentence, after convicting him of three counts of inciting to racial hatred.[4] The verdict stated that the defendant gave religious lessons at the Al Aqsa Mosque and outside it, videotaped the lessons and posted some of them on YouTube. In one instance the defendant said that the Jewish Holocaust occurred due to their corruption, and because they prepared "special bread" for Passover through the abduction of children, placing them in a barrel full of needles and making bread using their blood.

From the viewpoint of law enforcement, incitement on the social media poses unique challenges:

1. Impartial law enforcement

Incitement over the social networks enables communication across borders and security fences. The physical location and actions dominant in criminal activity lose much of their significance. This means that you might not be able to indict the most serious offenders, only those that are under your jurisdiction. It is also the case that the pace and volume of the data are very high, making them hard to monitor, and placing heavy responsibility on the law enforcement monitors – for example – we have had a magistrate court judge release from custody a suspect in an incitement case, on the grounds that she has personally encountered FB pages with publications that are much worse than the alleged offenses of the suspect in the case.

2. Lack of material evidence

In the "old world," if inciting statements had been written on a wall or distributed in leaflets or given as a speech, typically there was material evidence one could have seized through an investigation. Incitement on social media is "short lived." It is easy to erase a post or even a whole FB page. Frequently hours after the arrest, we find the FB profile of the suspect erased. It is obvious that much of the incitement publications can be erased a few days after the publication, making it hard to detect and capture.

3. The inciters identity

The issue of "virtual identity" has many implications. In the context of our work against inciters, it can be difficult to reveal the true identity of the person owning the page or the website. At this point in time, in most cases the investigators do not need to use sophisticated technology in order to reveal the owners of the publications. However, we can be quite confident to assess that intense enforcement will lead to much more cautious and clever behavior by the inciters, including the use of virtual identities to camouflage the real people

4 Michael Bachner, *Muslim preacher jailed over inciting speeches at al-Aqsa*, YNET NEWS, March 15, 2016, http://www.ynetnews.com/articles/0,7340,L-4778803,00.html.

behind the incitement publications. Thus, investigators will need the cooperation of private service providers that own the technological infrastructure or manage communications. Issuing warrants to these companies and obtaining information involves legal procedures, bureaucracy and at times substantive legal work that takes time and effort. When the suspect is under arrest, it is a challenge to accomplish this in the limited time available. Another challenge in this respect is websites or FB profiles operated by groups of people. When only some content constitutes incitement, it raises legal questions of mutual responsibility, co-conspiracy and collaboration.

4. Assessing the content of the publications – do they constitute an offense? This is certainly the most difficult challenge for the prosecution. The offense of incitement to violence and terror consists of three main elements. The first element is "publication." The second is the substantive content of the publication – a call to commit an act of violence or terrorism, or the publication of words of praise, sympathy or encouragement of an act of violence or terrorism. The third is the requirement that through the publication's content and the circumstances under which it was published, there is a tangible possibility that the publication will lead to committing an act of violence or terrorism.

The first element, in the context of our subject, raises no difficulty. Yet the second and third elements raise serious questions when we are required to judge specific publications. For example, regarding the second element, does a publication using the title "Shaheed" (roughly translated as martyr or saint) attached to a picture or name of a person that committed a terrorist attack, constitute an offense? Following serious debate, the Attorney General has decided in this case that if there are no additional words of praise, a publication of this sort is not an offense. A similar dilemma arose with regard to the term Intifada (roughly translated as "uprising"). Will a post saying: "The third intifada to protect El-Aksa is on its way" constitute an offense? In one case, after much deliberation, such a publication was included in the indictment, based on the context of other publications on the same FB page. Closely attached are dilemmas regarding the third element of "tangible possibility" (tangible is understood to be higher than probable but lower than "nearly certain"). According to the Supreme Court's ruling, this element does not require concrete factual evidence of either a poll or referendum among the relevant audience. It is to be assessed by the court according to the circumstances.[5] In practice, we seek to establish the number of people in the audience; in the context of FB, the investigators try to determine the number of followers and friends and the number of "likes" and responses to the inciting post. We also

5 RCA [request of criminal appeal] 2533/10 State of Israel v. Michael Ben-Horin (2011).

consider the use of hash tags as a means to expand the exposure of the publication. The traditional parameters of role and status in the relevant community or group are also paramount.

Another major parameter is the era and atmosphere in the relevant audience. When a tide of terror or violence erupts in a certain community, and the atmosphere is explosive, more people might be responsive to incitement. Contrary to that, in periods of relative calm, the same publication will have a much lower likelihood of moving people to acts of violence or terror. The temporal nature of publications on social media is also considered. A post that is months old is judged in the context of the time when it was published.

Due to the sensitivity of the incitement offences and their influence on freedom of speech, both directly as a limitation on what citizens are allowed to say and also indirectly as having a potential chilling effect on public discourse, great caution is required in the enforcement of these offenses. Law enforcement efforts in dealing with incitement are carefully monitored at different stages. Primarily, the Penal Law requires the approval of the Attorney General in order to file an indictment.[6] Accordingly, the monitoring of the law enforcement actions against inciters begin at the outset of these investigations. By the directive of the Attorney General, in order for the police to initiate an investigation on suspicion of incitement, preliminary approval is needed. This approval is granted by prosecutors in the State Attorney's Office only after careful examination of the materials brought by the police. In practice, a significant amount of publications are not approved for investigation. It should also be noted that the indictments prepared and authorized by the District Attorney are then reviewed by the Deputy State Attorney (Special Affairs) and by the State Attorney himself, before they are handed over to the Attorney General for approval.

Handling suspected offenses of incitement to violence, terror and racism, particularly in cyberspace, is not simple, both on the investigative level and on the prosecution level, because cases involving such offenses contain great complexity, both from a constitutional standpoint, from a legal – technological standpoint and from the public and social standpoints. However, the complexity has not deterred Israel's prosecutors from confronting this challenge. Rather, it has led to the development of investigative techniques, professional work procedures and closely observed policies by which the prosecution and other law enforcement agencies join hands to effectively confront a dangerous criminal phenomenon, guided by the light of Chief Justice Barak's words:

---

6 Israel Penal Law (5737–1977), s.123, https://www.nevo.co.il/law_html/Law01/073_002.htm.

> Protecting democracy requires the maintenance of freedom of expression. Maintaining freedom of expression requires protecting democracy. The use of the rhetoric of democracy and human rights as the basis for action that harms democracy and human rights is a true and tried recipe for the destruction of democracy from within. True, democracy recognizes the right of expression and demonstration of any person therein; it will do everything possible to respect this right, but democracy will not allow the rights it grants to be used to bring about self-destruction. Democracy must also be tolerant of the intolerant, but democracy should not allow in its tolerance its own destruction.[7]

7 CrimApp 5934/05 *Shai Malka v. the State of Israel* (2005).

The UN and Incitement

Anne F. Bayefsky

1 The UN Has No Definition of Terrorism

The UN has no internationally-agreed definition of terrorism, a fact that undermines its capacity to identify, condemn or prevent incitement to terrorism.

The UN's inability to define terrorism is a result of an ideological conflict between the 56 UN member states in the Organization of Islamic Cooperation (OIC) (and the subset of OIC states in the Arab League), and the remaining roughly 70% of UN members. OIC and Arab League states are parties, respectively, to the Terrorism Convention of the Organization of the Islamic Conference[1] and the Arab Terrorism Convention.[2] Both of these treaties define terrorism to exclude armed struggle for liberation and self-determination.[3] This claim purports to exclude from international delict violence directed against certain civilians, contrary to generally-accepted prohibitions of international humanitarian law. Thus, statements by countries that are party to these treaties, either condemning terrorism or incitement to terrorism, must be interpreted alongside their embrace of an exclusion clause at odds with international norms.

Furthermore, in the absence of a UN definition of terrorism, statements by UN officials, as well as resolutions and reports from UN bodies either

* I gratefully acknowledge the assistance of Sarah Willig and David Litman in the preparation of this paper.

1 Organization of the Islamic Conference (OIC), *Convention of the Organisation of the Islamic Conference on Combating International Terrorism*, July 1, 1999, Annex to Resolution No: 59/26-P.

2 League of Arab States, *Arab Convention on the Suppression of Terrorism*, April 22, 1998.

3 "Article 2(a). Peoples' struggle including armed struggle against foreign occupation, aggression, colonialism, and hegemony, aimed at liberation and self-determination in accordance with the principles of international law shall not be considered a terrorist crime." Organization of the Islamic Conference (OIC), *Convention of the Organisation of the Islamic Conference on Combating International Terrorism*, July 1, 1999, Annex to Resolution No: 59/26-P; "Article 2(a). All cases of struggle by whatever means, including armed struggle, against foreign occupation and aggression for liberation and self-determination, in accordance with the principles of international law, shall not be regarded as an offence." League of Arab States, *Arab Convention on the Suppression of Terrorism*, April 22, 1998.

 | DOI 10.1163/9789004359826_012

condemning terrorism or incitement to terrorism are inherently ambiguous, and intended to mean different things to different audiences.

In particular, a sizeable number of UN states maintain that incitement to terrorism specifically directed at Israelis is not even prohibited, and UN officials and bodies routinely either embrace that position or avoid contradicting it by intentionally using equivocal language.

2 The Role of the General Assembly

The definitional impasse at the United Nations over the meaning of terrorism has affected the ability of the UN General Assembly to tackle the issues of terrorism and incitement to terrorism in a number of ways.

Since 2000, the General Assembly has sought to adopt a comprehensive convention on international terrorism but been unable to do so.[4] The divergence of opinion between the members of the OIC and the rest of the General Assembly has been openly articulated by the chairman of the working group charged with drafting the comprehensive convention and by OIC states themselves during meetings of the Assembly's Sixth (Legal) Committee.

For instance, on November 13, 2015 the Chairman of the General Assembly working group circulated an oral report in which he named "the outstanding issues." He highlighted the OIC demand "to distinguish between acts of terrorism and the legitimate struggle of peoples under foreign occupation and colonial or alien domination in the exercise of their right to self-determination."[5]

Speaking on behalf of the OIC on October 3, 2017 at a General Assembly meeting, Saudi Arabia stated: "we reaffirm our determination to make every effort to reach a consensus agreement on the draft convention, by resolving the outstanding issues including those related to the legal definition of terrorism, particularly on the distinction between terrorism and the struggle for the rights of self-determination by people under foreign occupation and colonial or alien domination…"[6] In 2016, Iran told the General Assembly working group

4 *See*: "Ad Hoc and Special Committees Established on the Recommendation of the Sixth Committee," http://legal.un.org/committees/terrorism/.

5 Summary record of the 27th meeting of the Sixth Committee, General Assembly, November 13, 2015, A/C.6/70/SR.27. *See also* comments on "outstanding issues" and "the definition of terrorism" in the "Oral report of the Chairperson of the Working Group," Measures to eliminate international terrorism, Sixth Committee, General Assembly, New York, November 3, 2017.

6 Statement by Saudi Arabia on behalf of the OIC Group before the Sixth Committee of the General Assembly on Item 107 "Measures to eliminate international terrorism," New York, October 3, 2017.

that the comprehensive convention on terrorism should contain an "exclusionary element" in "the definition of terrorism" for "people which are fighting against colonial domination and alien occupation and against racist régimes in the exercise of their right of self-determination."[7]

The General Assembly adopted a "UN Global Counter-Terrorism Strategy" in 2006. But the Global Strategy does not contain a definition of the terror it is purporting to counter, or therefore, incitement to terrorism.[8] The Global Strategy includes a Plan of Action consisting of four "pillars." The first pillar is entitled "Measures to address the conditions conducive to the spread of terrorism." It attempts to shift the focus from the victims of terrorism to suggesting that those engaged in terrorism are themselves victims.[9] The focus of UN attention, quite purposefully, has moved away from so-called security-based counter-terrorism measures to prevention.[10]

The Global Strategy does mention incitement and specifically calls upon states: "To continue to work to adopt such measures as may be necessary and

7 United Nations General Assembly Sixth Committee Working Group on "Measures to eliminate international terrorism," Informal Consultations, New York, October 17, 2016.

8 So Lebanon continued to claim during the 2016 General Assembly's Global Counter-Terrorism Strategy Review: "When dealing with counter terrorism, we must also keep in mind that it should not be associated with other principles recognized under international law, such as the right to self-determination and to resist foreign occupation. In this regard, my delegation would like to denounce the attempts from one delegation to label the legitimate right to resist foreign occupation as terrorism…" United Nations General Assembly "Fifth Review of the United Nations Global Counter-Terrorism Strategy," UN Headquarters, New York, July 7, 2016.

9 "Pillar I. We resolve to undertake the following measures … (6) To pursue and reinforce development and social inclusion agendas at every level as goals in themselves, recognizing that success in this area, especially on youth unemployment, could reduce marginalization and the subsequent sense of victimization that propels extremism and the recruitment of terrorists." The United Nations Global Counter-Terrorism Strategy, A/RES/60/288, September 8, 2006.

10 Secretary-General's Remarks at the "Geneva Conference on Preventing Violent Extremism – The Way Forward," April 8, 2016: "The Plan of Action puts forward a comprehensive and balanced approach for concerted action at the global, regional and national levels. It is based on five inter-related points: Number one, we must put prevention first. Evidence shows that security and military responses **alone** cannot defeat this scourge. Sometimes such responses have proven to be counter-productive…" Bold added. A classic straw man, since no one has advocated security and military responses "alone." https://www.un.org/sg/en/content/sg/statement/2016-04-08/secretary-generals-remarks-geneva-conference-preventing-violent. *See also:* Human Rights Voices: http://www.humanrightsvoices.org/EYEontheUN/terrorism/?p=3366.

appropriate and in accordance with our obligations under international law to prohibit by law incitement to commit a terrorist act or acts and prevent such conduct."[11] There being no definition of terrorism, however, what would constitute incitement to commit a terrorist act is left indeterminate.

3 The Role of the Security Council

The UN Security Council has taken a highly selective approach to addressing terrorism and incitement to terrorism. The outlook is directly related to the absence of a UN definition of terrorism. For instance, though the Security Council is charged by the UN Charter with primary responsibility for maintaining international peace and security, it has never adopted a resolution mentioning the terrorist organization "Hamas."[12]

In fact, incitement and glorification of terrorism occurs at the Security Council itself and goes unchallenged by Council members. The Palestinian UN representative regularly sends letters to the Security Council, that in turn become official UN documents, labeling terrorists who have carried out attacks against Israelis as "martyrs."[13]

11 Pillar I (4), The United Nations Global Counter-Terrorism Strategy, A/RES/60/288, September 8, 2006.

12 Hamas is listed as a foreign terrorist organization by the United States and by the European Union, among others. "Designated Foreign Terrorist Organizations," U.S. Department of State, (since October 8, 1997); Council Common Position 2003/651/CFSP of 12 September 2003 updating Common Position 2001/931/CFSP on the application of specific measures to combat terrorism and repealing Common Position 2003/482/CFSP, 2003 O.J. L 229/42. The governing charter of Hamas, "The Covenant of the Islamic Resistance Movement," openly dedicates Hamas to genocide against the Jewish people. In its words: "the Islamic Resistance Movement aspires to the realisation of Allah's promise, no matter how long that should take. The Prophet, Allah bless him and grant him salvation, has said: 'The Day of Judgement will not come about until Moslems fight the Jews (killing the Jews), when the Jew will hide behind stones and trees. The stones and trees will say O Moslems, O Abdulla, there is a Jew behind me, come and kill him.' ...There is no solution for the Palestinian question except through Jihad... The Islamic Resistance Movement considers itself to be the spearhead of the circle of struggle with world Zionism ... Islamic groupings all over the Arab world should also do the same, since all of these are the best-equipped for the future role in the fight with the warmongering Jews." The Covenant of the Islamic Resistance Movement, August 18, 1988. Articles 7, 13, 32. Available at: http://avalon.law.yale.edu/20th_century/hamas.asp.

13 *See for example:* Identical letters dated October 20, 2008 from the Palestinian Observer to the United Nations addressed to the Secretary-General and the President of the Security

While Security Council press statements are regularly issued in response to high profile terror attacks throughout the world,[14] such statements are almost never issued when the terrorist attack is directed at Israel.[15]

Starting on November 13, 2015, the UN began to catalogue on its website the "UN response to acts of terrorism." Of the 72 Security Council Press Statements or Presidential Statements condemning a terrorist act logged on the UN site from November 13, 2015 to June 15, 2017, only two relate to terrorist attacks against Israel. During that same period of time, however, Palestinians perpetrated against Israelis 123 stabbing attacks, 144 shooting attacks, 51 vehicular attacks, and 1 vehicle bombing; as a result, 34 Israelis were murdered and 650

Council, A/ES-10/424-S/2008/667: "Names of martyrs killed by the Israeli occupying forces in the Occupied Palestinian Territory, including East Jerusalem* (from Wednesday, June 18, 2008, to Thursday, October 16, 2008) ... Monday, June 23, 2008 1. Iyad Radwan Khanfar 2. Tareq Jumaa' Abu Ghali." CNN reported on the June 23rd attack, for example: "Earlier Tuesday, the Israeli military said it killed a senior member of Islamic Jihad and another militant with him during a raid in Nablus, in the West Bank. The senior militant, Tareq Jumaa Ahmed Abu Ghali, opened fire at the Israeli soldiers as they tried to arrest him, according to the Israel Defense Forces. The soldiers fired back, killing Abu Ghali and the other militant, the IDF said." "Hamas: We want truce, despite rocket attacks," CNN, June 24, 2008, http://edition.cnn.com/2008/WORLD/meast/06/24/gaza.truce/index.html.

14 From January 2001 through June 2017, the Security Council issued 581 press statements condemning terrorism or violent extremism. Only 20 involved attacks against Israeli targets. (Compilation on file with author.) During that time, there have been thousands of terror and rocket attacks against Israelis. *See*: "Wave of terror 2015–2017," Israel Ministry of Foreign Affairs, June 18, 2017, http://mfa.gov.il/MFA/ForeignPolicy/Terrorism/Palestinian/Pages/Wave-of-terror-October-2015.aspx; "Suicide and Other Bombing Attacks in Israel since the Declaration of Principles (September 1993)," http://mfa.gov.il/MFA/ForeignPolicy/Terrorism/Palestinian/Pages/Suicide%20and%20Other%20Bombing%20Attacks%20in%20Israel%20Since.aspx ; "Victims of Palestinian Violence and Terrorism since September 2000," http://mfa.gov.il/MFA/ForeignPolicy/Terrorism/Palestinian/ages/Victims%20of%20Palestinian%20Violence%20and%20Terrorism%20sinc.aspx.

15 Israeli Ambassador to the United Nations, Danny Danon, told the Security Council on January 26, 2016: "During the past four months, Israelis have been stabbed in their homes, shot at in the streets, and run over by terrorists using cars as weapons. Over the course of this wave of violence, thirty people have been killed, and hundreds have been injured. During this period of time, the Council has adopted twelve resolutions, twelve, against terrorism, and condemned terrorist attacks in France, Sinai, Lebanon, Mali, Tunisia, Turkey, Iraq, Syria, Nigeria, Burkina Faso, Somalia, and Sudan. Not once were the lives of Israelis murdered by terrorists recognized by this Council. No condemnation, no expression of solidarity, not even a statement of concern." http://embassies.gov.il/un/statements/security_council/Pages/Danon-Security-Counil.aspx.

were wounded.[16] The UN's silence in the face of terrorism targeting Israel enables, and indeed encourages, further acts of incitement to terrorism, and terrorism itself.

In 2001, shortly following the 9/11 attacks, the Security Council created the "Counter-Terrorism Committee" (CTC) to be its lead agent on the subject of terrorism.[17] The CTC is comprised of exactly the same 15 Security Council member states. In 2005, the Security Council adopted an important resolution directly addressing incitement to terrorism. Among other things, Resolution 1624 directed the CTC to discuss with member states their efforts to prohibit and prevent incitement to terrorism.[18] In 2008, the Security Council requested the Executive Directorate of the CTC (CTED) to continue to support the CTC's work in the context of the prohibition and prevention of incitement to terror.[19]

The theory, however, is impeded by the highly opaque practice of the CTC and its associated UN secretariat, whose modus operandi is to avoid pointing fingers or naming names.[20] Although the CTC can elicit reports from member states, self-reporting bumped up against the absence of a UN definition of terrorism. Iran[21] and Syria[22] – both state-sponsors of terrorism[23] – were able to submit written reports to the CTC claiming that they were engaged in a vigorous campaign to combat terrorism. (Eventually such reports were no longer produced or made public.) And while the CTED can and does produce its own assessments of individual member states, the contents are not shared publicly. The names of countries which the CTED has visited are also

16 Wave of terror 2015–2017, Israeli Ministry of Foreign Affairs, http://mfa.gov.il/MFA/ForeignPolicy/Terrorism/Palestinian/Pages/Wave-of-terror-October-2015.aspx.

17 S/RES/1373 (2001).

18 S/RES/1624 (2005). The CTED has also issued general reports such as a: "Global survey of the implementation of Security Council resolution 1624 (2005) by Member States." S/2016/50, January 28, 2016. The UN Security Council preference is to have the CTED "identify and assess issues, trends and developments" *See*: S/RES/2395 (2017).

19 S/RES/1805 (2008).

20 In terms of terrorist organizations, rather than states, the exceptions are ISIL/Da'esh, Al Qaida, the Taliban and associated groups or entities.

21 Letter dated March 12, 2007 from the Chairman of the Security Council Committee established pursuant to resolution 1373 (2001) concerning counter-terrorism addressed to the President of the Security Council, S/2007/142, March 13, 2007.

22 Letter dated August 3, 2006 from the Acting Chairman of the Security Council Committee established pursuant to resolution 1373 (2001) concerning counter-terrorism addressed to the President of the Security Council, S/2006/612, August 4, 2006.

23 State Sponsors of Terrorism, U.S. Department of State, https://www.state.gov/j/ct/list/c14151.htm.

not always released.[24] It is worth noting that the absence of a definition of terrorism has not prevented the UN from creating an ever-expanding counter-terrorism bureaucracy.[25]

4 "Countering Violent Extremism"

The continuing clash over a UN definition of terrorism, and the shift in UN emphasis away from security-based counter-terrorism measures towards prevention, has pushed an alternative framework to the fore: "countering violent extremism" or CVE.

In late December 2015, UN Secretary-General Ban Ki-moon released a "Plan of Action to Prevent Violent Extremism." Far from leaving the definitional problem with "terrorism" behind, however, the Secretary-General saddled "violent extremism" with the same definitional yoke. At the very outset of the Plan, he announced:

> Definitions of "terrorism" and "violent extremism" are the prerogative of Member States… [T]his Plan of Action pursues a practical approach to preventing violent extremism, without venturing to address questions of definition.[26]

Why preventing a problem without defining it would be considered "practical" is hard to comprehend.

The CVE Plan of Action redirects attention away from the actual inciters and towards those responsible for responding to them. The Plan states, for instance:

> *Marginalization and discrimination*
>
> 26… [W]hen a country experiences insecurities such as scarce resources, and when one group, whatever its demographic weight, acts monopolistically in political and economic sectors at the expense of other

24 Country-specific "Preliminary Implementation Assessments" (PIA's) and "Detailed Implementation Surveys" (DIS) have not been made public.

25 *See* the elaborate Counter-terrorism Implementation Task Force (CTITF) "structure" chart, https://www.un.org/counterterrorism/ctitf/en/structure, and the Office of Counter-Terrorism (OCT) created in 2017. http://www.un.org/en/counterterrorism/.

26 Plan of Action to Prevent Violent Extremism, Report of the Secretary-General, A/70/674, para. 5, January 7, 2016.

> groups, the potential for intercommunal tensions, gender inequality, marginalization, alienation and discrimination increases, as expressed through restricted access to public services and job opportunities and obstructions to regional development and freedom of religion. **This, in turn, may incite those who feel disenfranchised to embrace violent extremism** as a vehicle for advancing their goals...[27]

In other words, pushing CVE as the primary counter-terrorism approach has enabled UN bodies, officials and member states, in effect, to flip the script – to excuse and promote terrorism under the guise of doing the reverse. As the representative of the organization of Islamic states (OIC) demonstrates, a UN conference on preventing violent extremism is perceived to be the right venue to explain and justify violent extremism:

> We're confronted with a faceless enemy, with no face or creed, which lurks in the shadows of fear and frustration, breeds on despair and disillusionment, and is fed by foreign occupation ... It's a manifestation of growing anger, hatred, and sense of helplessness against continuing wars, injustice, oppression, and the denial of fundamental freedom and rights, particular to those of Palestinians.[28]

Or in the words of Sudan (whose President has been indicted for crimes against humanity and genocide by the International Criminal Court) speaking at the same UN conference on preventing violent extremism: "Foreign occupation is

27 Bold added. The Plan continues: "50. I therefore recommend that Member States: ... (d) Strengthen the professionalism of security forces, law enforcement agencies and justice institutions; and ensure effective oversight and accountability of such bodies, in conformity with international human rights law and the rule of law. This may involve providing dedicated human rights training to security forces, law enforcement agents and all those involved in the administration of justice regarding the prohibition of incitement to hatred and, more broadly, respect for human rights within the context of measures taken to counter violent extremism and terrorism...," Plan of Action to Prevent Violent Extremism, Report of the Secretary-General, A/70/674, January 7, 2016.

28 Afshin Mehdiyev, Ambassador, Permanent Observer of the Organisation of Islamic Cooperation to the European Union in Brussels, Speaking at the "Geneva Conference on Preventing Violent Extremism – The Way Forward," April 8, 2016, United Nations Geneva, Human Rights Voices, http://www.humanrightsvoices.org/site/developments/?d=14885; *See* in general for the Geneva Conference, April 7–8, 2016, United Nations Geneva, https://www.un.org/counterterrorism/ctitf/en/geneva-conference-preventing-violent-extremism.

indeed the incubator, the main incubator that breeds terrorism and violent extremism."[29]

The President of the UN Human Rights Council in 2016 explained the shift from countering terrorism to preventing violent extremism by stressing: "efforts must be made to address the underlying grievances that foster violent extremism and terrorism."[30] It is a confounding message, since the "grievances" for subjecting innocent human beings to terrible harm are far more likely to be rooted in gross intolerance, xenophobia, antisemitism and an aversion to democracy and liberty.

The UN's quite deliberate emphasis on CVE has worked to marginalize, and even to minimize, the legitimacy of combating incitement to terrorism and violent extremism through self-defense measures and lawful security responses.

5 A Statistical Analysis of UN Resolutions on Incitement

No doubt, the UN has addressed the subject of incitement and produced an increasing number of resolutions dealing with the issue over time.[31] The context in which the subject is introduced has varied, and more specifically has concerned incitement to:

- terrorism or violent extremism
- other forms of violence
- hatred or discrimination
- genocide
- piracy
- abuse of women
- torture, and
- forced migration.

29 Speaking at the "Geneva Conference on Preventing Violent Extremism – The Way Forward," April 8, 2016, United Nations Geneva, Human Rights Voices, http://www.humanrightsvoices.org/site/developments/?d=14885.

30 Choi Kyonglim (South Korea). Inputs from the President of the Human Rights Council to the 2016 High Level Political Forum: the Work of the Human Rights Council in relation to the 2030 Agenda for Sustainable Development, June 6, 2016, http://www.ohchr.org/Documents/Issues/MDGs/Post2015/Contribution2016HLPF.pdf.

31 Database on file with author.

Sometimes these forms of incitement have been addressed concurrently, such as resolutions that address both:

- hatred or discrimination *and* terrorism or violent extremism
- hatred or discrimination *and* other forms of violence.

And in some cases, the kind of incitement is unspecified; instead, incitement appears in a list alongside terrorism or violent extremism (and occasionally other offences).

From January 1, 2000 to December 31, 2016, 322 resolutions of the UN's primary bodies (the Security Council, the General Assembly, the Economic and Social Council (ECOSOC), and the Human Rights Commission/Council) have dealt with incitement in one of the above contexts.

Examining the references to incitement more closely, the most common references take two forms: first, incitement in the context of hatred or discrimination *and* violence (violence that does not expressly involve terrorism or extremism) (117 resolutions), and second, incitement that is unspecified but appears in a list alongside terrorism or violent extremism (80). When incitement is addressed in the context only of terrorism and violent extremism (27), it is almost always by the Security Council. Where incitement is addressed only in the context of hatred or discrimination (36), it is almost always by the General Assembly and the Human Rights Commission/Council.

Of the 322 total number of resolutions addressing incitement in any form (2000–2016), the majority – 171 – do so in a country-specific context. Of incitement references in a country-specific context, 97 (57%) – the majority – are in the context of the Israeli-Palestinian conflict.[32] Another 12 resolutions that address incitement refer to terrorist organizations, specifically Al Qaeda, the Taliban, ISIL, al-Nusra, Al-Shabaab – but never refer to specific Palestinian terror organizations, including Hamas.[33]

Of the 97 resolutions on incitement in the context of the Israeli-Palestinian conflict, 32 criticize Israel for incitement and "provocation." Incitement and provocation are always joined in the Israel-Palestinian case so as to manufacture a reason – an Israeli provocation – for any possible Palestinian transgressions.

32 The remainder are divided as follows: Côte d'Ivoire – 23, Somalia – 12, South Sudan – 10, Democratic Republic of the Congo – 7, Burundi – 5, Libya – 4, Myanmar – 3, Guinea – 3, Yemen – 2, Eritrea – 1, Eritrea & Djibouti & Somalia – 1, Iraq – 1, Sudan – 1, Central African Republic – 1.

33 The breakdown is: Al Qaeda (12),Taliban (3), ISIL (6), the Al-Nusrah Front (3), (and 1 resolution mentions Al-Shabaab along with the states of Eritrea, Djibouti and Somalia).

Another 62 resolutions mention incitement without a perpetrator and then go on to single out Israel for other alleged offences, either in a list of violations that include incitement (25), or in a different part of the resolution (37).

To sum up, 97% (94 of 97) of resolutions having something to do with incitement that are situated in the Israeli-Palestinian context specifically point fingers at Israel. And 3 incitement-related resolutions (all from the Security Council) are neutral as to the perpetrator, and either point to violations without directly naming the culprits or demure from specifying other violations. The Palestinian Authority and Hamas are never directly named as the perpetrators of incitement in any of the UN incitement resolutions from the four key UN bodies since the year 2000, including incitement to terrorism or violent extremism.

Naming names matters. In the words of the Nuremberg Tribunal "crimes against international law are committed by men, not by abstract entities."[34]

In reality, Palestinian incitement to terrorism is systematic, continuous, public and well-documented. It includes: propagating official praise for terrorists and terrorist acts; indoctrinating children to admire and emulate violent behavior in schools and camps; naming public facilities and monuments after terrorists; and making payments to terrorists and their families.[35]

But at the United Nations, the facts are turned on their head: efforts to confront, condemn and stop Palestinian incitement to terrorism have resulted in condemnations of Israel for incitement. The credibility and efficacy of the UN's treatment of incitement has been seriously diminished by its continuing preoccupation with, and discrimination against, Israel.

6 Examples of Incitement to Terrorism at the UN

In the absence of a definition of terrorism or incitement to terrorism, statements praising terrorist acts – including the violent murder of women and

34 Judgment: The Law of the Charter, Judgment of the International Military Tribunal for the Trial of German Major War Criminals, Nuremberg, September 30 and October 1, 1946. Available at: http://avalon.law.yale.edu/imt/judlawch.asp.

35 *See for example*: Palestinian Media Watch, https://www.palwatch.org/; The Middle East Media Research Institute (MEMRI), https://www.memri.org/; Palestinian terror and incitement, Israeli Ministry of Foreign Affairs, http://mfa.gov.il/MFA/ForeignPolicy/Terrorism/Palestinian/Pages/default.aspx; *See infra*, Erez Padan, *Fighting Incitement: The Work and Practice of the Israeli Prosecution 2014–2016;* Amos N. Guiora, *Inciting Terrorism on the Internet: The Limits of Tolerating Intolerance.*

children – are considered acceptable forms of speech at the UN. Not only are they allowed to proceed uninterrupted, they are translated and broadcast globally via UN webcasts and archived in the UN's online library to serve as a permanent resource.[36]

Incitement to terrorism is a constant feature of the statements of the chief Palestinian UN representative Riyad Mansour. For instance:

- "We are so proud that in this popular uprising, that has started almost two months ago, that the backbone of this uprising are the youth of Palestine."[37]
- "The Palestinians were resisting as much as they could in every place, including Jerusalem. It was their duty and they would continue doing so. Their efforts would be intensified further…"[38]

---

36 Incitement to terrorism and violent extremism at the UN includes: praising acts of terrorism, denying terrorist acts constitute terrorism, and demonizing Israelis such that they are perceived as appropriate targets of terrorist acts. For instance, on November 29, 2016, Ecuador told the General Assembly (quoting Fidel Castro): "We repudiate … Nazism against the Jewish people, but I cannot think of anything more similar in our contemporary history than the eviction, persecution, and genocide which, today, is being carried out by Imperialism and Zionism against the Palestinian people." November 30, 2016, General Assembly, http://webtv.un.org/meetings-events/general-assembly/watch/question-of-palestine-and-situation-in-the-middle-east-50th-plenary-71st-session-general-assembly/5230852623001#full-text.

37 Mansour was speaking at the opening of an exhibit at UN Headquarters on the occasion of the UN's "International Day of Solidarity with the Palestinian People," November 23, 2015. He was referring to what is known as the 'knife intifada' that began in September 2015 and which has resulted (to mid-June 2017) in the death and injury of almost 1,000 Israelis. Wave of terror 2015–2017, Israel Ministry of Foreign Affairs, http://mfa.gov.il/MFA/ForeignPolicy/Terrorism/Palestinian/Pages/Wave-of-terror-October-2015.aspx. Palestinian officials who incite Palestinian children to perpetrate acts of terrorism, including murder, instrumentalize these children to violate the most fundamental right of all: the right to life. Moreover, Palestinian adults who encourage Palestinian child terrorism violate one of the most fundamental rights of the child, namely, the right not to take part in armed conflict or hostilities. "Report on Palestinian Child Terrorists: Children Who Kill and Their Adult Enablers," Human Rights Voices, August 1, 2016, http://www.humanrightsvoices.org/site/documents/?d=15409. Second report, "Palestinian Child Terrorists: Children Who Kill and Their Adult Enablers," August 1, 2017, Human Rights Voices, http://www.humanrightsvoices.org/assets/attachments/documents/Palestinian_child_terrorists_August_1_2017_final.pdf . From September 2015 to August 1, 2017, at least 99 Palestinian minors have been involved in 79 separate terrorist attacks that have killed six and injured 38 Israelis.

38 Mansour was speaking at a UN meeting on May 13, 2014. "International Meeting on Question of Jerusalem Focuses on City's Current Realities." UN Press Release, May 16, 2014, http://www.humanrightsvoices.org/site/developments/?d=12172.

- "Legitimate resistance to the occupation has been criminalized as terrorism."[39]

In 2017, Palestinian representative Mustafa Barghouti[40] told a meeting at UN Headquarters: "Popular Palestinian resistance to occupation and apartheid, brings back the same basic principles that we used in preparation and in initiating the First Intifada … Popular resistance means using all forms of possible resistance… The most important form is the popular resistance on the ground by Palestinians."[41]

Across UN bodies, incitement to terrorism appears in various forms: the attempt to exclude Israeli beneficiaries from prohibitions of terrorism, the promotion of "armed struggle" and "all available means" as solutions to the Israeli-Palestinian conflict, and the glorification of violence. For instance, Lebanon told a General Assembly meeting in 2016: "my delegation would like to denounce the attempts from one delegation to label the legitimate right to resist

39 Mansour was speaking at the UN General Assembly, November 23, 2015, http://webtv.un.org/meetings-events/general-assembly/watch/general-assembly-62nd-plenary-meeting-70th-session/4628796224001 .

40 Member of the PLO Central Council, the Palestinian Legislative Council, and General Secretary of the Palestinian political party, the Palestinian National Initiative.

41 Statement by Mustafa Barghouti at the UN "Forum to Mark Fifty Years of Occupation," Panel III, UN WebTV, June 30, 2017, http://webtv.un.org/meetings-events/watch/part-2-un-forum-ending-the-occupation-creating-the-space-for-human-rights-development-and-a-just-peace-civil-society-forum/5489727870001. The first "intifada," or violent uprising, took place from 1987 to 1993. It involved "more than 3,600 Molotov cocktail attacks, 100 hand grenade attacks and 600 assaults with guns or explosives" against both Israeli soldiers and civilians. This period was also marked by significant violence among Palestinians themselves in a so-called "intrafada." Israel's Wars & Operations: First Intifada (1987–1993), Jewish Virtual Library, http://www.jewishvirtuallibrary.org/first-intifada. The false "apartheid" charge is wielded as a tool to delegitimize a Jewish state. The reality is that Arab citizens of Israel are judges on the Supreme Court, ambassadors representing Israel in foreign affairs, and Israeli Cabinet Ministers. They have their own political parties in Israel's parliament. In short, they have more democratic rights in Israel than in any Arab state. At the same meeting, Saeb Erekat, Secretary-General of the Palestine Liberation Organization told the UN audience: "Hamas and the PFLP [Popular Front for the Liberation of Palestine] are not terrorist organizations." Erekat was speaking as an invited panelist at the UN "Forum to Mark Fifty Years of Occupation," Panel I, UN Web TV, June 29, 2017, http://webtv.un.org/meetings-events/.watch/1st-meeting-un-forum-ending-the-occupation-the-path-to-independence-justice -and-peace-for-palestine/5487676788001. Both Hamas and the PLFP are listed as foreign terrorist organizations by the United States and by the European Union, among others.

foreign occupation as terrorism..."[42] Qatar told the Human Rights Council in 2017: "We need to distinguish between terrorism and the legitimate resistance, which is the right of peoples who suffer from occupation and oppression."[43] In 2016, Rima Khalaf, head of the UN's Economic and Social Commission for Western Asia, repeated an old General Assembly resolution that reaffirmed, quote, the inalienable right of all peoples to self-determination, freedom, and independence. And also reaffirmed the legitimacy of their struggle for liberation from colonial and foreign domination and alien subjugation by all available means, including armed struggle."[44] NGO "Just Vision" – invited to speak by a UN committee as the sole representative of "civil society" – told a meeting at UN Headquarters in 2016: "Next year ... marks 30 years since the First Intifada, the most disciplined and sustained civil resistance movement in Palestinian history."[45]

7 Conclusion

The UN's inability to define terrorism has significantly impeded attempts by its leading bodies, the Security Council and the General Assembly, to combat incitement to terrorism – occurring even within the walls of the UN. The absence of a definition has obstructed the UN's capacity to identify and condemn the perpetrators of incitement, and to develop adequate solutions to this growing and dangerous phenomenon. The UN's more recent emphasis on "countering violent extremism" has tended to have a counter-productive result: focusing on the alleged "grievances" of terrorists, rather than recognizing and

42 Statement of Lebanon, UN General Assembly Global Counter-Terrorism Strategy Review, July 7, 2016, http://statements.unmeetings.org/media2/7659406/lebabon.pdf#sthash.rooqbLi7.dpuf.

43 Statement of Qatar at the 34th session of the UN Human Rights Council, UN Web TV, March 3, 2017, http://webtv.un.org/meetings-events/human-rights-council/watch/clustered-id-sr-on-protection-of-human-rights-and-on-cultural-rights-14th-meeting-34th-regular-session-human-rights-council/5345702700001#full-text.

44 Second Committee of the General Assembly (Economic and Financial Committee), 22nd meeting. 71st General Assembly, October 25, 2016, http://webtv.un.org/watch/second-committee-22nd-meeting-71st-general-assembly/5185037761001 (at 37:25–38:01).

45 Suhad Babaa, Executive Director, NGO "Just Vision," was the UN's chosen representative from "civil society." Statement given at the "Special meeting in observance of the International Day of Solidarity with the Palestinian People," November 29, 2016, http://webtv.un.org/watch/committee-on-the-exercise-of-the-inalienable-rights-of-the-palestinian-people-380th-meeting/5228422141001.

responding appropriately to the inexcusable intolerance that drives incitement in the first place.

Israelis find themselves in the crosshairs of incitement to terrorism – facilitated by the UN itself. But the effort to legitimize an Israeli target, and the UN's inability or unwillingness to stop Israeli-focused incitement in its midst, has had a negative impact on the institution's power to prevent incitement to terrorism directed anywhere. In an effort to justify the targeting of civilians deemed to stand in the way of supposed "liberation," the members of the Organization of Islamic Cooperation (most of which are not free democracies) continue to block the adoption of a universal definition of terrorism that would apply to all civilians. Such inequality violates the essence of international humanitarian and human rights law. And the same group of states continue to thwart the adoption of a comprehensive convention on international terrorism that would serve all people without discrimination. The impasse, and the enabling of incitement, leaves today's UN part of the problem instead of the solution.

PART 3

Incitement, Terrorism and War

Targeting Speech in War

Rachel VanLandingham

1 Issue

What measures does the law of armed conflict allow in response to individuals who provoke and/or urge violence, those who engage in the distribution of propaganda, and those who engage in recruiting activities?

I. When does a *person* committing incitement become targetable (lawfully subject to lethal/destructive force) under the law of armed conflict? What about a person recruiting on behalf a party to an armed conflict, or distributing propaganda/advocating for them?
II. When does *a communication system* itself (such as a radio station, TV station, or internet website), used to communicate such incitement, become a lawful target for destruction or jamming during an armed conflict?

2 Background

The law of armed conflict, also known as international humanitarian law or the law of war, applies only during an armed conflict. While the geography of the battlefield is not a clearly settled issue, the on/off switch of this body of law is the existence of an armed conflict. The below analysis assumes the existence of an armed conflict, either an international armed conflict (between two or more nation-states) or a non-international armed conflict (between one or more non-state armed groups and a nation-state, or solely among non-state armed groups). The basic targeting rules are the same for both types of conflicts as a matter of customary international law.

Assuming an extant armed conflict, the law of armed conflict allows both people and objects to constitute valid targets, that is, be subject to lethal force and destruction through attack, although the legal rules for valid target identification differ depending on category (person versus object).[1]

1 Once an object's or person's target validity is established (a process called target verification), a proportionality analysis must be conducted if, in the destruction of the validated target, civilians or civilian property are expected to be harmed.

 | DOI 10.1163/9789004359826_013

3 Discussion

3.1 *People as Targets*

The foundational principle of the law of armed conflict, distinction, divides the world of war into civilians and belligerents, and only the latter may be directly targeted.[2] Belligerents may be targeted based on their *status as such*, regardless of their conduct at the time of targeting, unless they are incapacitated due to surrender, wounds, etc.[3] Civilians may only be the object of attack if and when they are "directly participating in hostilities,"[4] a legal term of art that restricts direct targeting of civilians to a temporal period in which they are involved in military operations in rather specific ways.

3.1.1 Belligerents

Given that belligerents may be targeted based on their status as such, it is critical to flesh out belligerency criteria (given the obvious incentive for placing one in that category). Traditionally, belonging to/membership in an armed group that fights on behalf of a party to the armed conflict has conferred belligerent status. Minus medical and religious personnel, all members of a nation-state's armed force are belligerents based primarily on the allegiance owed to their sovereign state that such membership represents,[5] and not necessarily the function they perform (for example, a U.S. Army soldier who is a cook is

---

2 This essay uses the term "belligerents" in its broadest sense to indicate persons engaged in hostilities in an armed conflict on behalf of a party to the conflict. Belligerent status for purposes of targeting differs from combatant status; the latter exists during an international armed conflict and confers combatant immunity (the privilege to wield violence that is shielded from criminal prosecution) as well as prisoner of war status upon those who qualify by, *inter alia*, wearing distinctive emblems, carrying arms openly, and obeying the law of armed conflict. Geneva Convention Relative to the Treatment of Prisoners of War, art. 4 August 12, 1949, 75 U.N.T.S. 135 [hereinafter Geneva Convention III].

3 Protocol Additional to the Geneva Conventions of August 12, 1949, and relating to the Protection of Victims of International Armed Conflicts (Protocol I), art. 41(2)(a)–(c), June 8. 1977, 1125 UNTS 3 [hereinafter Additional Protocol I] *Hors de combat* is recognized as constituting customary international law and applicable in all armed conflicts. *See:* Yoram Dinstein, THE CONDUCT OF HOSTILITIES UNDER THE LAW OF INTERNATIONAL ARMED CONFLICT (2nd ed. 2010).

4 Additional Protocol I, art. 51(3).

5 *See:* Rachel VanLandingham, *Meaningful Membership: Making War A Bit More Criminal*, 35 Cardozo 79 (2013) ("Membership, because of its inherent agency relationship of command, demonstrates a submission of self to the central, overarching violent purpose of the group.").

a belligerent as much as a soldier who is a sniper).[6] Members of armed forces are typically identifiable as targets based on their uniforms, proximity to other members, or function, for example.

However, identifying an individual's status in today's asymmetric conflicts against non-state armed groups is often challenging. Individuals belonging to non-state organized armed groups typically fail to wear uniforms or otherwise distinguish themselves from civilians, and intentionally hide amongst them. Notwithstanding a lack of black letter treaty law for determining status of non-state entities, membership in a belligerent non-state armed group, or at least in their armed wing, is considered by both the United States and ICRC sufficient to trigger belligerent status.[7] For example, the latest edition of the United States Department of Defense (DOD) Law of War Manual states that:

> Being part of a non-State armed group that is engaged in hostilities against a State is a form of engaging in hostilities that makes private persons liable to treatment in one or more respects as unprivileged belligerents by that State. Being part of a non-State armed group may involve formally joining the group or simply participating sufficiently in its activities to be deemed part of it.[8]

Not all nation-states recognize this broad concept of belligerency, which includes both those "privileged" by the law to engage in hostilities (by meeting the criteria established in Article 4, Geneva Convention III) and those considered "unprivileged" belligerents (who fail to meet the Article 4 criteria yet are belligerents based on membership in non-state armed groups). Such states classify all individuals not meeting the traditional "combatant" status articulated in the Third Geneva Convention as civilians, and hence only targetable

6 Department of Defense Law of War Manual, June 2015, updated May 2016, at 216, para. 5.8.1, https://www.documentcloud.org/documents/2997317-DoD-Law-of-War-Manual-June-2015-Updated-May-2016.html [hereinafter DOD Law of War Manual] ("The organization's hostile intent may be imputed to an individual through his or her association with the organization.").

7 Int'l Comm. of the Red Cross, *Interpretive Guidance on the Notion of Direct Participation in Hostilities under International Humanitarian Law* (May 2009), https://www.icrc.org/eng/assets/files/other/icrc-002-0990.pdf ("All armed actors showing a sufficient degree of military organization and belonging to a party to the conflict must be regarded as part of the armed forces"; and "members of organized armed groups belonging to a non-State party to an armed conflict cease to be civilians ... and lose protection against direct attack, for as long as they assume their continuous combat function.").

8 *See:* DOD Law of War Manual, at 158, para. 4.18.4.1.

when directly participating in hostilities, either as a member of an organized armed group, or individually. In contrast, the ICRC allows that if one is continually engaged in hostilities on behalf of an armed group, then one is a member of that group who can be targeted based on such status. The American category for those who can be lawfully targeted during an armed conflict based on their status is broader than the ICRC's position and some states, in that it does not restrict the category of belligerents solely to those continually engaged in hostilities, which is the ICRC position.[9] The United States logically believes that identifying a belligerent based on membership in a non-state armed group involves a different process than that required to identify a civilian who has temporarily lost their targeting immunity (the ICRC basis). For the U.S., one can be a member – either actual or constructive – of a non-state armed group and hence a belligerent based on a holistic functional determination.

The United States employs such a functional test to determine said membership in order to overcome the fact that membership in a terrorist organization (non-state armed group) can be frustratingly opaque. This functional test focuses on one's role within a particular group; the individual's role in the group signifies the individual's subordination to that group's command and control, making them eligible for membership and thus belligerent status (hence making them a valid military target). Various criteria are relevant for making this membership determination: evidence of formal membership, such as swearing an oath of allegiance to a group; data that reveals the individual's integration within the group's command structure (he/she acts at the direction of the group and/or gives such direction); whether the person performs a function for the group that is analogous to one performed by a member of a state's armed force; evidence of direct participation in hostilities, and other factors that would reasonably "demonstrate an individual's integration into the armed group."[10]

Although a critical factor in determining group membership includes whether the person is part of a command structure, that is, obeys instructions from other group members or gives such instructions, such "chain of command" information is often lacking. As a result, membership is also determined by reviewing engagement in activities such as "training with al-Qaeda or taking

9 DOD Law of War Manual, at 224, para. 5.9.2.1 ("The U.S. approach has been to treat the status of belonging to a hostile, non-State armed group as a separate basis upon which a person is liable to attack, apart from whether he or she has taken a direct part in hostilities.").

10 Geoffrey S. Corn et. al., THE LAW OF ARMED CONFLICT: AN OPERATIONAL APPROACH 154 (2012). *See also:* DOD Law of War Manual, at 218–220.

positions with enemy forces,"[11] attending non-state armed group training camps, or staying in such groups' guesthouses.[12] The United States has also labeled conduct such as "accompanying the brigade on the battlefield, carrying a brigade-issued weapon, cooking for the unit, and retreating and surrendering under brigade orders"[13] as indicative of membership.

The United States views traditional "combat support" activities as indicative of membership, to include intelligence gathering, communications support, maintenance, cooking, logistics, provision of legal services, media relations, etc.; in fact, it views performance of *any* of the functions which correspond to traditional roles within states' armed forces as information that may indicate membership.[14] The key to finding that someone is a member of or belonging to a group (and hence dons a mantle of belligerency), regardless of individual function, is some indication of specific intent to further the group's violent aims. Such intent can be inferred from sufficient group integration:

> An individual who is integrated into the group such that the group's hostile intent may be imputed to him or her may be deemed to be functionally (i.e., constructively) part of the group, even if not formally a member of the group. The integration of the person into the non-State armed group and the inference that the individual shares the group's intention to commit hostile acts distinguish such an individual from persons who are merely sympathetic to the group's goals.[15]

3.1.1.1 *Propaganda as an Indicator of Membership?*

So when does an individual's on-line recruiting and propaganda activities on behalf of a group such as ISIS indicate that one is a member of, or belongs to, ISIS such that one is considered a belligerent and therefore targetable? Interestingly, although the Department of Defense's top lawyer stated in late 2012 that "[o]ur enemy does not include anyone solely in the category of activist,

11 *See* :Harold Hongju Koh, Legal Advisor, U.S. Dep't of State, Address to the Annual Meeting of the American Society of International Law: The Obama Administration and International Law (March 25, 2010), http://www.state.gov/s/l/releases/remarks/139119.htm.

12 *Al-Bihani v. Obama*, 590 F.3d 866, n.2 (D.C. Cir. 2010).

13 *Id.* at 872–873.

14 DOD Law of War Manual at 218, para. 5.8.3.1; 220, para. 5.8.3.2. *See generally:* W. Hays Parks, *Part IX of the ICRC "Direct Participation in Hostilities" Study: No Mandate, No Expertise, and Legally Incorrect*, 42 N.Y.U. J. Int'l L. & Pol. 769, 813–820 (2010).

15 DOD Law of War Manual at 219, para. 5.8.3.2.

journalist, or propagandist,"[16] the DOD Law of War Manual states unequivocally that "Non-State armed groups sometimes use their members for propaganda or other media activities, and such personnel are not precluded from being considered unprivileged belligerents."[17]

This question is not theoretical, as highlighted in the recent New York Times story detailing drone killings by the United States of several men who appeared to be recruiters as well as hackers ("social media experts") for ISIS.[18] Critically, while there are few details in the article indicating the targeted men's level of integration into ISIS, it described them as having "given a far-reaching megaphone to Islamic State propaganda and exhorted online followers to carry out attacks in the West."[19] It appears that one of the targets coordinated at least one plot to kill a specific person; this likely constituted acting as part of ISIS's command structure as well as performing a role analogous to that in a traditional armed force, if data demonstrated that this individual was in communication with known ISIS members. Using the DOD Law of War Manual's terms, it appears that these men's actions indicated that they shared "the group's intention to commit hostile acts" and hence were distinguishable from "persons who are merely sympathetic to the group's goals."

The above discussion indicates that one's recruiting and propaganda activity on behalf of a group like ISIS may in fact indicate membership in the group because, if "[b]eing part of a non-State armed group may involve ... simply participating sufficiently in its activities to be deemed part of it,"[20] then their participation in its recruiting and propaganda machine may deem them part of that organization, and qualify them for what the DOD Law of War Manual deems "constructive belonging" to the armed group.[21] However, additional facts indicating that a person is part of the group's command structure or otherwise a member is integral to placing the targeting decision on quite solid ground.[22] Otherwise the assessment would have to be considered under the following section as an individual act of direct participation.

16 Jeh Johnson, Gen. Counsel, U.S. Dep't of Defense, Address at the Oxford Union: The Conflict Against Al Qaeda and its Affiliates: How Will It End? (November 30, 2012) (transcript http://www.lawfareblog.com/2012/11/jeh-johnson-speech-at-the-oxford-union/).

17 DOD Law of War Manual, at 173, para 4.24.1.2.

18 Adam Goldman and Eric Schmitt, *One by One, ISIS Social Media Experts Are Killed as Result of F.B.I. Program*, NEW YORK TIMES, November 24, 2016.

19 *Id.*

20 *See:* DOD Law of War Manual at 158, para. 4.18.4.1.

21 *Id.*

22 For example, the United States government highlighted U.S. citizen Anwar al-Awlaki's operational and leadership roles in an official legal memo regarding the U.S. decision to place

3.1.2 Civilians & Direct Participation in Hostilities

In contrast with status-based targeting of belligerents, the law of armed conflict only allows civilians to be targeted when they are directly engaged in hostilities; by definition, they are typically presumed to be non-participating. Only a civilian's current participation in hostilities (which includes some time immediately prior to and immediately after the qualifying activity) at the time of targeting can legally justify such attack. Once they stop engaging in such conduct, they can no longer be targeted. The law provides no exact test for determining what activities constitute direct participation, although the International Committee of the Red Cross (ICRC) has promulgated a somewhat useful three-part test consisting of three criteria: threshold of harm, direct causation, and a belligerent nexus.[23]

There is widespread agreement that certain common activities associated with armed conflicts fall within that category, and particular ones that definitely do not. For example, conduct equaling direct participation, according to military manuals, includes "taking up arms or otherwise trying to kill, injure or capture [an] enemy …."[24] The Israeli Supreme Court has labeled direct participation as someone "who collects intelligence on the army … who transports unlawful combatants to or from the place where hostilities are taking place … who operates weapons … or supervises their operation, or provides service to them, be the distance from the battlefield as it may."[25] It also described activities that it did *not* consider to be direct participation, such as "a person who sells food or medicine to an unlawful combatant … who aids the unlawful combatants by general strategic analysis, and grants them logistical, general support, including monetary aid … who distributes propaganda supporting those unlawful combatants."[26]

The Israeli court's conclusions above echo the common understanding that a "mere contribution to the general war effort (e.g. supplying foodstuffs to

---

him on a kill list. *See:* https://www.washingtonpost.com/r/2010-2019/WashingtonPost/2014/06/23/National-Security/Graphics/memodrones.pdf?tid=a_inl.

23 Int'l Comm. of the Red Cross, *Interpretive Guidance on the Notion of Direct Participation in Hostilities under International Humanitarian Law* 46 (May 2009).

24 William H. Boothby, THE LAW OF TARGETING 157 (2012).

25 *Public Committee against Torture in Israel v. Government of Israel*, HCJ 769/02, Judgment (December 13, 2006). *See generally*: Michael N. Schmitt, *Deconstructing Direct Participation in Hostilities: The Constitutive Elements*, 42 N.Y.U. J. Int'l L. & Pol. 697, 708 (2010) (discussing this landmark Israeli HCJ decision).

26 *Id.*

combatants)" is not considered direct participation in hostilities,[27] because entire societies are involved at some level in modern war. The principle of distinction would be eviscerated if such general efforts allowed civilians to be targets.[28] However, direct participation is not limited solely to acts involving lethal force, either.[29] The U.S. Department of Defense (DOD) Law of War Manual states that "[t]aking a direct part in hostilities extends beyond merely engaging in combat and also includes certain acts that are *an integral part of combat operations* or that effectively and substantially contribute to an adversary's ability to conduct or sustain combat operations."[30]

3.1.2.1 *When Does Speech Constitute Direct Participation in Hostilities?*

As the Israeli Supreme Court concluded, mere distribution of propaganda, that is, disseminating material advocating on behalf of a party to an armed conflict, is widely believed to *not* constitute direct participation in hostilities. Using the same logic, neither is other general support that often comes in the form of speech, such as training, recruiting, and financing.[31] The reason is that these types of activities lack direct causation of harm to the enemy. Whereas "transmitting tactical targeting information for an attack" (by oral speech or by pointing to a building to highlight where the enemy is hiding in order to indicate their position for attacking forces, for example) *is* considered direction participation in hostilities, general exhortations urging others to join the fight, or specific guidance on how to use one's particular choice of weapon lack such a direct link to harm.[32]

---

27 Yoram Dinstein, THE CONDUCT OF HOSTILITIES UNDER THE LAW OF INTERNATIONAL ARMED CONFLICT 28 (2nd ed. 2010).

28 *Prosecutor v. Strugar*, Case No. IT-01-42-A, Appeals Judgment, ¶ 176–179 (Int'l Crim. Trib. for the Former Yugoslavia July 17, 2008).

29 The ICRC Commentary to Additional Protocol I provides, "[t]o restrict this concept [of direct participation in hostilities] to combat and to active military operations would be too narrow, while extending it to the entire war effort would be too broad, as in modern warfare the whole population participates in the war effort to some extent, albeit indirectly."

30 DOD Law of War Manual at 224, para. 5.9.3.

31 The ICRC's Interpretive Guidance suggests that such activities do not constitute direct participation: "Thus, recruiters, trainers, financiers and propagandists may continuously contribute to the general war effort of a non-State party, but they are not members of an organized armed group belonging to that party unless their function additionally includes activities amounting to direct participation in hostilities." *Interpretive Guidance on the Notion of Direct Participation in Hostilities under International Humanitarian Law* 48 (May 2009).

32 *Id.*

In other words, without more, simply exhorting other civilians to carry out terrorist attacks is likely insufficient to transform a civilian into a lawful target during armed conflict. The same characterization applies to someone who provides strategic direction for so-called "lone wolf' attacks, despite doing so to aid a party to an armed conflict: the causal link necessary for direct participation in hostilities *may* be missing. However, the closer an individual gets to causing direct harm, the closer they get to crossing into direct participation. For example, if a civilian urges other civilians on the street to stand in front of a weapons cache in an attempt to shield that weapons cache from imminent enemy targeting, and the person urging knows or should know that they will likely listen to him, direct harm to the enemy's military efforts is likely to result. Hence such urging, in such a narrow circumstance, could constitute direct participation in hostilities.[33]

This level of directness can be applied to recruiting, for example, which is typically not considered direct participation in hostilities due to a similar causal lack of direct harm. As the ICRC explains, "only where persons are specifically recruited and trained for the execution of a predetermined hostile act can such activities be regarded as an integral part of that act and, therefore, as direct participation in hostilities."[34] It is unclear what type of situation the ICRC was envisioning with this statement, but it demonstrates that the closer one gets on a spectrum of proximity to the actual causation of harm either to the enemy's military operations or to those protected by the law, the closer that activity is to direct participation in hostilities.

3.2 *Objects as Targets*

3.2.1 Basic Criteria

Since the principle of distinction requires that civilians be spared from the effects of military operations to the greatest extent feasible, it follows that civilian objects, like civilians themselves, cannot be the object of attack. Instead, the law of armed conflict allows only military objectives to be targeted. The difficulty here lies in determining which category a particular object falls into at a particular time, given that this determination is highly contextual. Similar to

---

33 Whether the persons actually serving as shields are themselves directly participating in hostilities depends on whether they voluntarily assumed such positions, knowing the purpose of that assumption. They would not be considered directly participating if they did not know they were acting as such, or if their actions were not voluntary.

34 *Interpretive Guidance on the Notion of Direct Participation in Hostilities under International Humanitarian Law* 53 (May 2009).

the direct participation in hostilities analysis above, there are both easy cases, and then there are the more challenging ones.

When dealing with objects and not people, the accepted definition of lawful military objective has two required elements: "those objects which by their nature, location, purpose or use make an effective contribution to military action and whose total or partial destruction, capture or neutralization, in the circumstances ruling at the time, offers a definite military advantage."[35] These two prongs must be cumulatively met, although if an object makes an effective contribution to military action its destruction or neutralization (denial of use by the enemy) will almost always offer "a definite military advantage" to the opposing party. However, the latter is broader than only denying such contribution, and is one that takes the larger war effort into account; military advantage refers "to the advantage anticipated from an attack when considered as a whole, and not only from its isolated or particular parts."[36]

What constitutes a military objective depends on the context. Some objects will almost always be considered military ones: for example, tanks and other weapons systems, military barracks, military command and control systems, or military headquarters. That is, such objects "used directly by the armed forces" are by their nature military objectives, and their destruction or neutralization is presumed to offer the required military advantage.[37] Other objects are those that are typically civilian, but based on location, purpose or use are considered military objectives instead. For example, focusing on the "use" criteria, "using" a children's elementary school to house soldiers logically transforms it into a lawful military objective for such time as that use continues.[38] Similarly, if a "location" such as a bridge outside of a major city contributes to military action as a potential route of enemy maneuver, it falls within the lawful military objective category because of its projected contribution to military action. "Purpose" refers to future intended uses, such as a civilian airport whose runways can be easily used by enemy forces in the future, or the Autobahn in Germany whose intended future use is as a means to move military force and supplies.

35 Additional Protocol I, Article 52.

36 DOD Law of War Manual, at 211, para. 5.7.7.3; *See also:* Yoram Dinstein, THE CONDUCT OF HOSTILITIES UNDER THE LAW OF INTERNATIONAL ARMED CONFLICT 94 (2nd ed. 2010)(military advantage "is not limited to tactical or local gains.").

37 AP I, Commentary. *See also:* DOD Law of War Manual, at 209, para. 5.7.6.1.

38 The required proportionality analysis if there is a risk that civilians or civilian objects will be harmed in the attack is a separate inquiry than the threshold determination of military objective prior to targeting.

While the DOD Law of War Manual states that purpose "means the intended or possible use in the future,"[39] the DOD General Counsel recently clarified that this means that a determination has been made that the enemy is *planning* to use the object for military purposes.[40] This makes sense, because if an object can be transformed into a military objective simply because it is "possible" that it could be used by the enemy for military purposes, then the distinction between military and civilian objects would be eviscerated, as almost every object could "possibly" contribute to military action.

3.2.2 Communications & Broadcasting Systems[41]

Command, control and communication systems related to running a war – used by the military (armed forces) – are non-controversially considered military objectives by nature, along the same lines as weapons systems.[42] That is, broadcasting facilities are military objectives if they are "integrated into" the opposing military's or armed group's command, control and communications systems, because they are part of the military.[43]

For example, the 1954 Hague Convention for the Protection of Cultural Property implies that broadcasting stations are valid military objectives; it describes special protection given to cultural property as long as it is "at an adequate distance from any important military objective constituting a vulnerable point such as, for example, ... [a] broadcasting station."[44] Additionally, the ICRC Commentary to AP I's definition of military objective provides a list of objects generally considered to be military objectives during armed conflict; it includes "installations of broadcasting and television stations; telephone and telegraph exchanges of fundamental military importance."[45]

---

39 DOD Law of War Manual, at 209, para. 5.7.6.1.

40 Jennifer M. O'Connor, *Applying the Law of Targeting to the Modern Battlefield (As Prepared)*, New York University School of Law, New York, November 28, 2016, https://www.justsecurity.org/34977/applying-law-targeting-modern-battlefield%E2%80%8E-full-speech-dod-general-counsel-jennifer-oconnor/.

41 Communications systems here refer to means of communication, in contrast with the term of art, "lines of communication" which classically refers to the transportation and supply routes (roads, railway lines) that an armed force uses to replenish and sustain itself; lines of communication are typically considered lawful military objectives.

42 Yoram Dinstein, THE CONDUCT OF HOSTILITIES UNDER THE LAW OF INTERNATIONAL ARMED CONFLICT, 97 (2nd ed. 2010).

43 W.J. Fenrick, *Targeting and Proportionality during the NATO Bombing Campaign against Yugoslavia,* 12 E.J.I.L. 489, 496 (2001).

44 Article 8.

45 ICRC Commentary to Additional Protocol I.

Furthermore, even if not fully integrated, the "use" criteria in the definition of military objective would transform such a facility or system into a military objective *if* it is being used at the time to contribute to military action; hence what "makes an effective contribution to military action" needs to be dissected. Does civilian use of a civilian radio or TV station, or internet site, to distribute propaganda on behalf of an armed group make an effective contribution to military action? The DOD Law of War Manual defines such contribution as a broad one regarding the general prosecution of the war, one that need not require any direct or proximate link to military operations; instead any "effective contribution to the war-fighting or war-sustaining capability of an opposing force is sufficient."[46] Using this expansive interpretation – which is a controversial one – one could argue that a civilian internet site disseminating propaganda on behalf of ISIS makes an effective contribution to military action because of its recruiting effect, and therefore is a lawful military objective.[47]

However, pure propaganda (defined as "information, especially of a biased or misleading nature, used to promote or publicize a particular political cause or point of view"[48]) lacks a nexus to military action, and therefore by itself it does not fit into either the traditional understanding of making an effective contribution to military action, nor the United States' controversially expansive take on that term.[49] However, if one can show that such propaganda has a recruiting effect, the calculus changes. Similar rationale applies to using such broadcast stations or modes of communication to disseminate incitement;[50] if such advocacy is likely to produce an effective contribution to military action,

46 DOD Law of War Manual, at 210, para. 5.7.6.2.

47 The recent DOD General Counsel speech indicates that DOD may be retreating from such an expansive position regarding war-sustaining activities, at least with respect to targeting Islamic State oil production and money. ("[W]e do not believe categorically that we can target any and all cash or revenue-generating objects simply because of their nature. Rather, we consider each potential target on a case-by-case basis and evaluate it in light of the information we have available, in order to assess whether it meets the definition of a military objective. This is no different than any other target.") Jennifer M. O'Connor, *Applying the Law of Targeting to the Modern Battlefield (As Prepared)*, New York University School of Law, New York, November 28, 2016, https://www.justsecurity.org/34977/applying-law-targeting-modern-battlefield%E2%80%8E-full-speech-dod-general-counsel-jennifer-oconnor/.

48 *See:* https://en.oxforddictionaries.com/definition/us/propaganda.

49 *See:* W.J. Fenrick, *Targeting and Proportionality during the NATO Bombing Campaign against Yugoslavia,* 12 E.J.I.L. 489, 496 (2001), discussing the WWII International Military Tribunal of Hans Fritsche, in which the tribunal distinguished between pure propaganda and that designed to incite war crimes.

50 *See generally:* Fenrick, at 496.

such as civilians blockading roads to impede enemy action, then the "effective contribution to military action" of such a broadcasting system is clear. The devil is truly in the details.

Since such contribution encompasses a wide range of behavior, a facility or system used to incite war crimes could arguably fall under an effective contribution to military action, if such war crimes confer a benefit to the enemy. For example, one expert has argued that *Radio Milles Collines* in Rwanda, which was used in 1994 to incite genocide, would be a lawful target based on a duty to prevent such a serious crime.[51] In the context of an armed conflict, one could also view such incitement as effectively contributing to enemy military action because the incitement's end result benefitted the opposing party, thus making it a lawful military objective.

It is critically important to note here that determining the legality of a target is only the first step; if civilians or civilian property are likely to be harmed in the destruction or neutralization of that target, a proportionality analysis must be conducted according to the law of armed conflict. Therefore, if an internet site such as Twitter is determined to be a lawful military objective because an armed group belonging to a party to an armed conflict is using it to communicate with other members and to recruit, any attack to destroy, disable or neutralize Twitter would have to be analyzed in light of the obligation to refrain from attacks in which the expected civilian harm would be "excessive in relation to the anticipated military advantage gained."[52] If such harm were likely, the attack would be prohibited by the law of armed conflict due to the "excessive" impact on the use of Twitter by uninvolved civilians.

As mentioned above, an additional interesting issue is whether or not all communications systems (ones currently being used for civilian purposes) that *could* be used by an armed group or military are *also* lawful military objectives because of their purpose, even if not instrinsically military or being so used at the time. According to the DOD General Counsel's recent remarks, if such systems are considered to be *planned* for future use by the enemy, and not just of speculative *possible* use, then by their purpose they would indeed be considered valid military objectives.

The DOD Law of War Manual seems to address this specific issue in a straightforward, affirmative manner: "[c]ommunications objects, such as facilities, networks, and equipment *that* could *be used* for command and control of military operations or intelligence gathering, have often been regarded

51 *Id.*

52 Additional Protocol I, Article 51(b)(5).

as military objectives."[53] But analogous to the manual's use of "possible" in its definition of purpose, this phrase "could be used" should be understood to relate to those facilities and systems in which there is objective information to support their planned – that is, intended – future use by the opposing military or armed group. The manual cites as support the 1999 NATO bombing of a state-owned TV studio in Belgrade; in fact, NATO had generically stated that along with military forces, command and control facilities, and other traditional military objectives, "media and broadcasting systems" were also deliberate objects of attack.[54] Yet looking at the context of that armed conflict, this broadcasting station was state-owned, and hence the intended future use by the state's military of such a broadcast system was implicated.

3.3 *Defining Attack: Jamming & Disrupting vs. Destroying*

A final relevant question concerns the definition of attack per the law of armed conflict; it leaves for another day what constitutes an armed attack (or other use of force) which may trigger a state's right to self-defense under the *jus ad bellum*.[55] According to Additional Protocol I, attacks are "acts of violence against the adversary, whether in offence or defence."[56]

The 1999 NATO bombing of a state-owned TV studio in Belgrade, described above, is a classic example of an "attack" per the law of armed conflict in that it was an "act of violence." At its simplest, if an act does not cause violence, it is not at attack, and the type of weapon used is irrelevant to this effects-based analysis. If NATO had used electronic jamming of the Belgrade TV studio to block its broadcasts for a few days, instead of bombing the facility and physically destroying it, this jamming would not have been considered an "attack" regulated by the above prohibitions regarding military objective, proportionality, and precautions, although such operation would arguably be constrained by the principles of humanity and military necessity.

---

53 DOD Law of War Manual, at 213, para. 5.7.8.2.

54 W.J. Fenrick, *Targeting and Proportionality during the NATO Bombing Campaign against Yugoslavia*, 12 E.J.I.L. 489, 495 (2001).

55 The United States believes that certain uses of force, even ones that do not constitute an armed attack, can trigger its inherent right to self-defense under the *jus ad bellum*, despite the limitation of self-defense in Article 51, UN Charter, to only armed attacks. *See:* DOD Law of War Manual, at 991, 16.3.3.1 ("[t]he United States has long taken the position that the inherent right of self-defense potentially applies against any illegal use of force. Thus, any cyber operation that constitutes an illegal use of force against a State potentially gives rise to a right to take necessary and proportionate action in self-defense").

56 Additional Protocol I, Article 49(1).

Whether an act constitutes an attack is particularly relevant in the cyber world. The DOD Law of War Manual acknowledges that "if the physical consequences of a cyber attack constitute the kind of physical damage that would be caused by dropping a bomb or firing a missile, that cyber attack would equally be subject to the same rules that apply to attacks using bombs or missiles."[57] According to the Tallinn Manual, a NATO-sponsored international treatise on the international law applicable to cyber operations, a "cyber attack is a cyber operation, whether offensive or defensive, that is *reasonably expected to cause injury or death to persons or damage or destruction to objects*" (emphasis added).[58]

The U.S. military lists factors that it believes indicate non-attack cyber operations, such as "whether the operation causes only reversible effects or only temporary effects."[59] It finds that the following cyber operations are not attacks: "defacing a government webpage; a minor, brief disruption of internet services; briefly disrupting, disabling, or interfering with communications; and disseminating propaganda"; it also concludes that the law of armed conflict's rule of military necessity applies, though without explaining why and how.[60] Using these definitions, cyber operations that temporarily disable a particular website, for example, and do not damage or destroy hardware or software would not considered attacks by the law of armed conflict. Such operations could therefore be taken against a civilian website, for example, during an armed conflict without regard to many of the law of armed conflict's prohibitions regarding attacks – although other bodies of international and domestic law may be relevant, such as the international law of neutrality.

As applied to the original queries this brief paper opened with, cyber operations that temporarily disrupt a particular Twitter account, for example, would not amount to an "attack" per the law of armed conflict, and therefore could be taken against accounts otherwise protected by the civilian cloak of immunity. The law of armed conflict principle of military necessity could be met, if one agrees that it applies, by a finding that such Twitter account was contributing

57 DOD Law of War Manual at 988, para. 16.2.1.

58 Michael N Schmitt (ed), TALLINN MANUAL ON THE INTERNATIONAL LAW APPLICABLE TO CYBER WARFARE (CUP 2013), http://www.ccdcoe.org/249.html, Rule 30, at 91–92.

59 DOD Law of War Manual, at 996, para. 16.5.2.

60 *Id.* Without explanation, the DOD Law of War Manual also finds that the general principles of the law of armed conflict apply to non-attacks, and even creates a brand-new legal rule for such non-attacks: "even if a cyber operation is not an 'attack' or does not cause any injury or damage that would need to be considered under the proportionality rule, that cyber operation still should not be conducted in a way that unnecessarily causes inconvenience to civilians or neutral persons." *See id.*

to recruitment for the enemy, for example, or inciting violence against a party to a conflict. Similarly, if one found that the law of armed conflict's requirement regarding feasible precautions is relevant to such a cyber operation, its targeted nature against one account (versus shutting down the entire Twitter site) would indicate that such precautions have been taken. However, this author is not convinced that the entire Twitter website could not be lawfully (per the law of armed conflict) disrupted for a temporary period, if deemed militarily necessary. Such a cyber operation would not constitute an "attack" because it would lack the consequential effect (damage to or destruction to objects) required,[61] and there is no "inconvenience" prohibition in the law of armed conflict, despite the DOD Law of War Manual's claim otherwise.

---

61 However, a minority view expressed in the Tallinn Manual finds that destruction of data could constitute an attack; that is, "interference with functionality that necessitates data restoration, while not requiring physical replacement of components or reinstallation of the operating system, qualifies as an attack. For these Experts, it is immaterial how an object is disabled; the object's loss of usability constitutes the requisite damage." *See:* Tallinn Manual at 93, para 11.

Criminal and Military Incitement Response Tools: Prosecution and Security Detention

Geoffrey S. Corn

1 Criminal Law and The Limits on Prevention

1.1 *Commonly Available Offenses and Their Limits*

In the U.S. and common law tradition, incitement to violence is traditionally addressed through the modality of criminal law. It is an axiom of the common law that any person who encourages another person to engage in criminal misconduct is guilty as if he or she committed the criminal act. Historically, the person inciting the criminal misconduct was treated either as a principal in the second degree (if present at the scene of the crime), or an accessory before the fact (if not present at the scene of the crime). Archaic pleading and jurisdictional constraints on holding such individuals accountable led to widespread reform of theories of complicity liability, resulting in a general notion of accomplice liability that today permeates criminal statutes.

Accomplices are charged and prosecuted with the criminal misconduct committed by the principal and, as such, the "accomplice" act is not a crime in itself, but a mode of criminal liability. As a result, use of accomplice liability prosecution as a "preventive" measure to deal with incitement is significantly compromised, because liability is contingent on proof that the incited party actually attempted or committed the offense the inciting party intended.

Other offenses do, however, provide a more effective option for preventing the consequences of incitement, specifically the inchoate offenses of solicitation and conspiracy. Unlike reliance on a theory of complicity for an attempted or completed crime of violence resulting from incitement, these are stand-alone offenses that do not require the incited party to actually attempt or commit a subsequent crime of violence. Instead, an individual inciting unlawful violence could be convicted based on evidence that he or she communicated the encouragement (solicitation) to another party with the intent that an offense be committed. Conspiracy is another inchoate offense that does not require proof that the actual object of the conspiracy was attempted or committed, although there must be proof of an actual agreement to commit such an offense, either express or implied.

These criminal law "tools" have obvious limits as an effective means of preventing incitement to violence. First, the alleged misconduct must fall within

 | DOI 10.1163/9789004359826_014

the scope of criminal jurisdiction. When incitement occurs outside the territorial jurisdiction of a given state – for example in the context of an extraterritorial military operation – the criminal laws of that state may not be applicable. Second, even when the incitement falls within the scope of a state's criminal jurisdiction, proof that the inciting party acted with the specific criminal intent (purpose) to encourage others to engage in unlawful violence is an essential requirement for conviction under any of these theories of criminal liability. Finally, successful prosecution will often require identifying the party who was the target of the incitement in order to meet the burden of proving the requisite criminal act associated with each offense (that the party attempted or committed a crime for purposes of accomplice liability; that the party received a communication to commit a crime for purposes of solicitation; that the party entered into an agreement to commit a crime for purposes of conspiracy).

The protection of speech as a form of expression also adds complications to proof of criminal *mens rea* (required mental state) in relation to incitement. Although freedom of expression does not immunize speech that falls within the scope of the offenses and modes of liability addressed above, defendants may certainly assert that their "expressive motive" contradicts allegations of intent to bring about a subsequent criminal act. This was a central issue in the criminal prosecution of Omar Abdel-Rahman, known as "The Blind Sheikh." Rahman was convicted of, *inter alia,* seditious conspiracy in violation of the U.S. federal criminal code.[1] His sermons provided primary evidence of his conspiracy with other defendants who planned to conduct a range of terrorist attacks in the New York City area. These sermons clearly encouraged the planned terrorist attacks. On appeal, Rahman argued that because he was acting in his capacity as an Iman, his speech was protected by the First Amendment. The Second Circuit Court of Appeals rejected this argument, noting that the First Amendment did not protect individuals from criminal sanction when the evidence establishes their speech is intended to solicit violence.[2] Specifically, relying on a line of Supreme Court precedent, the court noted, "[T]hese cases make clear that a line exists between expressions of belief, which are protected by the First Amendment, and threatened or actual uses of force, which are not."[3]

Nonetheless, any defendant charged with soliciting, conspiring, or as an accomplice to a crime of violence based on incitement will have the opportunity to challenge the sufficiency of the evidence to prove the requisite specific

1 *See: United States v. Rahman*, 189 F.3d 88 (2d Cir. 1999).
2 *Id.*
3 *Id.* at 115.

criminal intent based on the alleged statements. To that end, an assertion that the statements were intended as a legitimate form of expression, and not intended to procure commission of an act of violence, will always complicate issues of sufficiency of proof.

Incitement obviously is closely related to acts of terrorism, and yet these traditional criminal offenses and modes of liability remain the primary tool in the U.S. criminal law arsenal to address incitement to engage in terrorism. Indeed, it seems somewhat perplexing that incitement is not more directly addressed in the primary terrorism prevention law enacted by Congress, the criminal prohibition against providing material support to terrorism. While the definition of material support is quite broad, it does not seem broad enough to cover incitement of terrorism violence without linking that incitement to one of the offenses addressed above.

There is no obvious impediment to congressional expansion of the definition of material support to include incitement to engage in terrorist violence on behalf of a foreign terrorist organization. Few would dispute the logic of punishing someone who engages in incitement as an accomplice to the incited terrorist crime if the evidence establishes an intent to encourage that crime. But prevention is ill served by this accomplice theory. This is because culpability is contingent on an attempted or completed terrorist offense. Solicitation is more expansive and therefore potentially more effective as a prevention tool, although the need to prove the completed communication to the solicited party presents its own evidentiary challenges. There seems to be no rational reason why incitement to commit acts of international terrorism could not be included within the definition of providing material support to terrorism. Because incitement will often result in activities committed to advance the objectives of a terrorist organization, it certainly provides support for that organization.

1.2 *Service Providers*

Subjecting service providers to criminal sanction for facilitating incitement may seem like a logical and necessary preventive measure, but it will almost always run afoul of basic doctrines of criminal responsibility. The profit motive associated with providing a service will frequently undermine the ability to prove the requisite specific intent necessary to punish a service provider as an accomplice or a co-conspirator, even when there is evidence indicating the service provider knew of the potential criminal use of the service. Some jurisdictions recognize a limited solution to this problem, treating the combination of knowledge of the criminal use and evidence of excessive or unusual profit as sufficient to support a finding of the requisite *mens rea* for accomplice or co-conspirator liability. However, this method of imputing criminal intent to a service provider is infrequently utilized, and absent evidence of a shared "stake in the venture" inferred from unusual or excessive profit, will almost never be effective.

Interestingly, the material support to terrorism offense may provide a more viable basis to prosecute a provider of services to an individual inciting terrorism than the actual individual engaged in the incitement. Because services are expressly included within the definition of material support, proof that the services were knowingly provided to a designated foreign terrorist organization would satisfy the requirements of the statute. However, prosecution would require sufficient evidence to satisfy this *mens rea* element: that the individual utilizing the service was known to the provider to be associated with a foreign terrorist organization and inciting activities on behalf of that organization. To my knowledge, no such prosecution has been initiated to date.

1.3 *Extending Criminal Prohibitions beyond the Borders*

Any assessment of the viability of using criminal law as a weapon in the counter-incitement arsenal must assess the permissible scope of state criminal jurisdiction. As a general proposition, international law does not anticipate an unrestricted projection of criminal laws by states outside their borders. Instead, well-recognized principles of criminal jurisdiction establish the accepted conditions of such extension.

In US practice, these international legal principles guide judicial assessment of permissible jurisdictional scope, but are not dispositive. Congress may extend US criminal law to any person in any location, and so long as congressional intent to do so is clear, courts may not invalidate that jurisdiction. However, when a criminal statute does not clearly indicate its intended jurisdictional scope, courts will presume Congress intended that scope to align with these principles of international law.

Any attempt to criminalize terrorism incitement outside the United States would therefore implicate international law jurisdictional principles. Like other extensions of US criminal law outside the territory of the United States, Congress may explicitly indicate jurisdictional predicates. For example, prohibiting incitement to commit acts of terrorism by or against US nationals, or incitement to commit acts of terrorism in the United States would be consistent with other extraterritorial extensions of US criminal law. Each of these situations would also align with existing principles of international law. A more complicated situation would arise if the United States sought to criminalize incitement to terrorism outside the United States when neither the defendant, the victim, nor the effect was connected to the United States. Because it is unclear whether terrorism falls within the scope of the "universal" principle of jurisdiction, it would be essential that Congress indicate its intent to extend law to such crimes.

1.4 *Conclusion*

This cursory review highlights the limits of reliance on criminal law to address, and especially to prevent incitement to violence. While criminal sanction plays an important function in the overall counter-terrorism strategy of the United States and many other nations, the "preventive" effect of criminal law is primarily the result of general deterrence. In contrast, incapacitation traditionally results following the commission of an offense. While crimes such as solicitation, conspiracy, and material support to terrorism do have a preventive effect beyond only deterrence, they remain primarily responsive in nature.

2 Military Operations and Potential Expanded Prevention Options

2.1 *The General Framework*

Preventing incitement in the context of a military operation will implicate potentially expanded authorities. These operations will generally fall into one of three categories: use of military to support civilian law enforcement efforts; United Nations authorized non-conflict peacekeeping operations; or situations of actual armed conflict bringing the law of armed conflict into force.

Military authority associated with the first type of operation – support to civil authorities – will be analogous to that exercised by civilian law enforcement agencies. In such situations, the military may bring unique resources and capabilities to the operation, but the nature of the mission will dictate the authority to use those capabilities. So, for example, a military unit may be equipped with enhanced surveillance capabilities, but use of the capability will be contingent on compliance with the same laws that govern law enforcement surveillance. Accordingly, while military assets may assist in the identification and potential apprehension of individuals engaged in incitement, incapacitation would remain within the exclusive purview of applicable domestic law.

Military authority associated with the second type of operation – a United Nations authorized mission – will be contingent on the nature of the Security Council mandate. Incitement prevention measures will rarely, if ever, be authorized in the context of peacekeeping authorized pursuant to Chapter VI of the Charter. The activities of military forces engaged in these missions are traditionally strictly limited to observation and monitoring. Use of force or any other measure of compulsion will be limited to action in self-defense in response to an actual or imminent threat to the UN forces. In contrast, missions conducted pursuant to Chapter VII of the Charter allow for a far more robust and aggressive use of military measures to achieve Security Council objectives. In this context, military action to prevent or disrupt incitement would be permissible so long as they were assessed as falling within the scope of the Security Council mandate, which in most situations will be quite general in nature (use of "all necessary means" or similar language).

Military authority associated with the third type of operation – an armed conflict – will be dictated primarily by the law of armed conflict. In these situations, actions to prevent or disrupt incitement to violence will normally be defined by two specific branches of this law: targeting law, and the law of belligerent occupation. The former branch will dictate when attacks, whether lethal or non-lethal, may be directed against individuals engaged in incitement and the platforms they utilize; the latter branch will dictate when preventive incapacitation measures may be used when a military commander physically controls the area of operations.

2.2 *The Law of Armed Conflict and Incitement Response*

As noted, response to incitement pursuant to the law of armed conflict implicates two primary branches of the law: targeting law and occupation law. Professor VanLandingham's excellent summary of targeting law as it relates to incitement comprehensively explains when use of lethal combat power may be directed against incitement and incitement platforms. I have nothing additional to add to her analysis, and incorporate it by reference.

Use of lethal combat power is not, however, the exclusive law of armed conflict authority implicated by the challenge of preventing or disrupting incitement to violence. When a military commander wrests from an enemy effective control over an area (with the exception of liberating national territory previously seized by an enemy), the law of belligerent occupation establishes the legal framework for governing and controlling that area. It is important to note that the "test" for occupation established by the law of armed conflict is intentionally *de facto,* as opposed to *de jure.* Even in areas where national authorities may be reluctant to acknowledge a situation of occupation (for example following the U.S. invasion of Panama in 1989), operational commanders will look to the law of belligerent occupation once they have asserted "effective control" over the area.

A fundamental authority granted to the occupying commander is the authority to implement measures to ensure both the safety of his forces and the safety and security of the local population. Article 43 of The Regulations Annexed to The Hague Convention (IV) of 1907 is the principal treaty basis for the exercise of this authority, and provides that, "The authority of the legitimate power having in fact passed into the hands of the occupant, the latter shall take all the measures in his power to restore, and ensure, as far as possible, public order and safety, while respecting, unless absolutely prevented, the laws in force in the country."[4] The 1949 Geneva Convention Relative to the Protection of Civilian Persons in Time of War includes a more comprehensive treatment of rights and obligations triggered by belligerent occupation, but this 1949 Geneva Convention in no way altered this basic security authority.

Accordingly, an occupying commander is vested with broad authority to both prevent and punish acts of incitement to violence, whether that violence is directed against the occupying force or members of the civilian population. An occupying commander is vested with authority to enforce existing penal law related to the obligation to ensure public safety and order; or, in the alternative, enact modifications or supplements to that law in the form of military orders and directives.[5] Accordingly, if the commander assesses that incitement activities are compromising public safety, this authority allows the commander to subject those responsible to criminal sanction for violating existing law, or to promulgate military orders that criminally proscribe incitement activities. Furthermore, either civilian or military tribunals may be used as the form to prosecute individuals alleged to violate either category of penal proscription (of course, these tribunals must ensure protection of fundamental rights).

To a certain extent, this penal response option is similar to a civilian peacetime penal response option. However, the authority to promulgate penal orders to supplement existing criminal law provides a substantial advantage to a military commander concerned with the consequence of incitement activity. However, the commander's response options are not, like her civilian law enforcement counterparts, limited to penal incapacitation. Instead, the express authority to utilize preventive administration measures is a powerful addition to the public and military safety response arsenal.

Geneva IV provides explicit authority to impose non-penal security measures in areas subject to occupation authority. While the law recognizes that civilians should be free from unnecessary restraints on liberty, it also allows a range of measures, culminating with administrative security internment, to address threats to the security of the occupying force resulting from civilian

---

4 Convention (IV) Respecting the Laws and Customs of War on Land and its Annex: Regulation concerning the Laws and Customs of War on Land, 187 CTS 227.

5 Geneva Convention Relative to the Treatment of Civilian Persons in Time of War, Art. 63, August 12, 1949, 75 U.N.T.S. 287 [hereinafter Geneva Convention IV].

activity.[6] Because the occupying power is responsible for establishing and preserving public order, this authority extends to these threats as well. Specifically, Article 78 provides that, "If the Occupying Power considers it necessary, for imperative reasons of security, to take safety measures concerning protected persons, it may, at the most, subject them to assigned residence or to internment."[7]

Note that assigned residence and internment are the "most" significant restraints on liberty authorized by Article 78. Accordingly, lesser restraints on liberty would also be justified. The only condition on imposition of such measures is a determination that a certain activity results in an imperative threat to security in the area subject to occupation authority. There is no rational reason why incitement activity would not fall into this category of security threats. Indeed, incitement to engage in violent or otherwise criminal activity represents a direct threat to military efforts to ensure public safety and security. Note, however, that incitement differs from mere propaganda or advocacy in that it consists of, at least in U.S. constitutional law, both intent to cause imminent lawless action and a reasonable likelihood that such action will actually be produced. Subjecting individuals assessed to be responsible for true incitement (an assessment that, unlike penal sanction, may be made based on a preponderance of information) to security internment would therefore be both authorized and logical. Article 78 does require compliance with certain basic procedures, and a periodic review of the necessity for continued internment, but it does not require a penal charge or conviction as a prerequisite.

3 Conclusion

States will often consider "shutting down" true incitement to violence a critical measure to protect the public and public officials from violence that might otherwise never materialize. Criminal laws, especially in the common law tradition, provide limited "preventive" effect to deal with this problem, although the expanding notion of counter-terrorism crimes may be expanding preventive use of penal sanction. Authority to engage in preventive action is much broader during armed conflicts, but still requires determinations of genuine necessity. All tools in the response arsenal should be continually assessed and, where necessary, rationally refined to ensure an effective balance between public security interests and the dangers associated with overbroad restrictions on legitimate non-violent expression.

6 *Id.* at Article 78.

7 *Id.*

Imminence Reconsidered

Asa Kasher

The purpose of the present paper is to reconsider the role played by imminence considerations in making decisions within the framework of fighting terrorism.

At the background of our discussion we are going to have two major assumptions. Ignoring such assumptions usually results in reaching conclusions that seem to us immoral or unethical.

Our first assumption is that decisions taken during fighting terrorism are made on grounds of ethical conceptions, whether explicit or implicit ones, which occupy certain positions on a basic spectrum of such conceptions. At one end of the spectrum we have some regular conception of police ethics as manifest in proper activity of police officers in domestic circumstances of enforcing law and order. At the other end of the spectrum we have some regular conception of military ethics as manifest in proper activity of men and women in military uniform during combat activity against enemy military forces in a regular war.

Ordinary conceptions of police ethics on the one hand and military ethics on the other hand differ from each other, naturally and significantly. Here is a major example of such a difference. Under combat conditions, when an important military target includes not only enemy combatants but a few enemy noncombatants, military ethics (as well as international law) allows attacking the target even though some collateral damage is foreseen, given that the proportionality condition obtains. On the other hand, if criminals hold hostages in some public setting, say a bank or a college campus, police ethics will not allow attacking the criminals when collateral damage is expected. The duty of police officers is to provide citizens with effective defense rather than killing them in an attack on criminals.[1]

Our second assumption is that under certain circumstances of fighting terrorism the proper ethics is a mixture of ingredients taken from both police ethics and military ethics.

1 Examples of cases where innocent citizens were killed by police officers during an attempt to overcome the criminals who took them as hostages are all examples of failures or of improper behavior in the first place. In a military activity, when the proportionality condition obtains, collateral damage is considered neither as a failure nor as a result of improper behavior.

 | DOI 10.1163/9789004359826_015

An illuminating example is that of targeted killing operations, as performed by Israel and some other democratic states. In military ethics of regular wars an ordinary target is an enemy combatant or a group of enemy combatants. The personal identity of the enemy combatant is seldom of any interest.[2] In targeted killing operations the identity of the targeted person is crucial. It provides one of the necessary conditions for a justifiable operation. On the other hand, expected collateral damage is not a compelling reason for aborting a targeted killing operation that satisfies the proportionality condition. This is a profound distinction between military ethics and police ethics. Thus, the ethical conception underlying targeted killing operations includes having a certain identified individual under consideration, on a par with police ethics, as well as permission to cause collateral damage if the proportionality condition obtains, on a par with military ethics of regular wars.

We turn now to a brief discussion of the condition of imminent danger within the framework of self-defense justifications of some operations.

Recall Daniel Webster's depiction of "imminent danger" in the famous *Caroline* case: justifying use of force in self-defense requires showing that the "necessity of that self-defense is instant, overwhelming, and leaving no choice of means, and no moment for deliberation."[3]

Within the framework of police ethics, the presence of imminent danger is a necessary condition of police actions of certain types. If danger is not imminent, the police officer in charge of the situation around the danger has time for deliberation. He can talk to the person who is the source of the danger under consideration, in an attempt to reach an agreement according to which the danger will be eliminated and the person's life is not going to be presently jeopardized by police officers. If for some reason talking to the person is not feasible, there is time for a choice of means less than lethal in order to solve the problem of danger without harming anyone. Only imminence justifies resort to no deliberation, just to the means at the police officer's disposal at the moment.

In military ethics of regular wars, imminence considerations usually play no role. An enemy military force is freely attackable even if it is not expected to cause any jeopardy in the foreseeable future. Unlike the line of thought within the framework of police ethics, here there is no interest in minimizing

2 The identity of an enemy combatant, such as a high ranking officer, could be relevant for proportionality considerations, but such operations rarely take place during usual combat with enemy forces.

3 Letter from Mr. Webster to Lord Ashburton, August 6, 1842, cited in Lori F. Damrosch et al., INTERNATIONAL LAW: CASES AND MATERIALS 923 (2001).

damages to the enemy forces by using alternative combat means. On the other hand, the possibility of putting an end to hostilities and replacing them by deliberations that are meant to lead to peace should always be considered, but it is a duty that belongs to the realm of politicians rather than that of people in military uniform.

What about circumstances that are governed by neither police ethics nor military ethics, namely those of fighting terrorism? Consider the case of a terrorist activity that is dubbed "suicide bombing" or "homicide bombing." The suicide/homicide bomber appears in the last stages of the terrorist operation. Actually, there is a long process of planning and preparations that takes place before the suicide/homicide bomber enters the scene. Here are some of the stages of that process: Terrorist A makes a decision to carry out an operation of that type. Terrorist B plans an operation. Terrorist C, "the pharmacist," collects explosives. Terrorist D, "the engineer," builds an explosive belt. Terrorist E recruits a driver F. Terrorist G recruits a suicide/homicide bomber H, etc.

If we use the notion of "imminence" the way it is put to usage by the police, on grounds of police ethics, the danger that justifies attacking in self-defense appears only when the bomber is approaching the mall in which he intends to push the button of explosion. Imagine that the whole process, from the action of A to the action of H takes place within a context of criminal activity. It would then indeed be justifiable for the police, on grounds of police ethics, to take everyone into custody, from A to H. Imagine that the whole process, again from A to H, takes place within a context of enemy military activity. It would then be justifiable for the military force, on grounds of military ethics, to attack everyone, from A to H. In the case of fighting terrorism, the familiar meaning of the notion of "imminent danger" will be replaced by a more reasonable one:

A danger is imminent, if all the following conditions obtain:

(a) If we do not do anything about it, the danger keeps getting closer to us; if we go on doing nothing about it, it will reach us;
(b) We ought to eliminate the danger, for a variety of reasons – constitutional, moral, ethical and other ones;
(c) We are now, for a short while, in a position of being able to eliminate the danger;
(d) We do not have any reason to assume that we are going to be, at a later stage, in the position of being able to eliminate the danger.

I suggest that fighting terrorism be done on grounds of an ethics that uses this notion of imminent danger rather than the classical one. When a suicide/homicide bomber operation is under consideration, it would mean that we may target the engineer, for example, and not wait until the bomber approaches the mall.

The ethics of fighting terrorism is, thus, again, a mixture of elements taken from police ethics and from military ethics of regular wars. On the one hand it is on a par with police ethics, when there is intelligence related to an ongoing attempt to carry out a suicide/homicide bombing operation, activities of self-defense have to focus on certain individuals, namely terrorists A to H. On the other hand, it is on a par with military ethics, using our notion of imminent danger and being allowed to cause collateral damage, when the proportionality condition obtains.

Returning to Daniel Webster's conditions, some consequences follow from our suggestion. First, the requirement that the danger be "instant" is simply wrong. It takes a while for an explosive belt to move from the "engineer" to the bomber, much beyond what is usually taken by "instant," but there is no reason to wait when our conditions of imminent danger obtain.[4] Second, the condition of the danger being "overwhelming" seems correct. Real jeopardy involves matters of life and death and is, under conditions of fighting terrorism, always overwhelming. Thirdly, the condition that the danger is "leaving no choice of means" is inappropriate. There obviously is a choice of means, but the problem is that there is no choice of positions in which we will be able to eliminate the danger. Fourthly and finally, the condition that there is "no time for deliberation" is also inappropriate. The crucial aspect of the situation is not that of the time left for the danger to knock on our doors, but rather the time we have for doing what is required for eliminating the danger. When the danger is evasive, since it is possible for intelligence to know the whereabouts of some of terrorists some of the time but not of all of them all the time, materialization time is much longer than elimination time. There is possibly ample time for talking, but almost no time for locating the terrorists before they drive to the gates of the mall.

US Army General Douglas MacArthur once said that "the history of failure in war can almost be summed up in two words: too late ... too late in realizing the mortal danger; too late in preparedness; too late in uniting all possible forces for resistance."[5] Importing the police ethics notion of "imminence" into the ethics of fighting terrorism will create yet another fatal case of "too late,"

---

4 There are depictions of "imminent danger" in military context in terms of how many days it would take for the danger to materialize. The figure 60, for example, has appeared in such a context. Our approach is more demanding, but morally and ethically preferable.

5 Edward T. Imparato, *Statement on Aid to Great Britain in Response to a request from William Allen White, Chairman of the Committee to Defend America by Aiding the Allies, September*

too late in elimination of danger. This is not going to be the right mixture of military ethics with police ethics.

In conclusion, a few summary points with respect to issues of incitement. First, a distinction between two different agents of incitement is important, namely (a) a citizen of the state, and (b) a person who is not a citizen of the state and is involved in incitement in the context of practically supporting terrorism against citizens of the state.

When the notion of "incitement" is understood as it is used in domestic cases, it is related to causing imminent danger, where "imminence of danger" is narrowly interpreted. The danger is real and overwhelming and it is expected shortly. Underlying such an interpretation is the justified need to find a balance between, on the one hand, protection of people against unjustifiable attacks and, on the other hand, protection of freedom of speech. Within the context of a democratic state such balances are always required, since liberties clash with each other and rights are always incompatible with each other if they are construed as absolute ones. Under circumstances of a clash between liberties and mutual incompatibility of rights, the crucial problem is where to draw the limits.

Such limits are not sacred, because often they are not purely conceptual but to some extent are rather contingent. The location of the limits depends on the dangers lurking beyond the borders. This is the reason why, for example, freedom of speech is delineated in different ways in seemingly similar democracies such as the U.S., Germany and Israel. Each of these states manifests a different portrayal of the dangers it is bound to face if the limits of freedom of expression are set elsewhere. A reconsideration of the present delineations of freedom of expression on grounds of a different understanding of "imminence" is therefore useful, namely according to the above-mentioned conception. The major issue is not how much time do we have until the danger materializes but rather what are the means at our resort that enable us to eliminate the danger.

In case incitement is a product of enemy persons who are not citizens of the state, issues of freedom of expression are much less significant and the application of this notion of "imminence" seems to be warranted. If we cannot protect the life of citizens when the jeopardy is caused by enemy incitement, because we cannot closely follow the process that leads from incitement to materialization of danger, then incitement must be stopped in a way that would be most effective and at least collateral damage costs.

16, 1940, GENERAL MACARTHUR, SPEECHES AND REPORTS 1908–1964, 122 (2000), https://books.google.co.il/books?isbn=1563115891.

PART 4

Emerging Issues and Challenges

Inciting Terrorism on the Internet: The Limits of Tolerating Intolerance

Amos N. Guiora

1 Introduction

The Internet is a limitless platform for information and data sharing. It is in addition, however, a low-cost, high-speed dissemination mechanism that facilitates the spreading of hate speech, including violent and virtual threats. Indictment and prosecution for social media posts that transgress from opinion to incitable hate speech are appropriate in limited circumstances. Several real-world examples discussed here help to explore when limitations on Internet-based hate speech are appropriate.

In October 2015, twenty thousand Israelis joined a civil lawsuit filed against Facebook in the Supreme Court for the State of New York. Led by the civil rights organization Shurat HaDin, the suit alleges Facebook allows Palestinian extremists to openly recruit and train terrorists to plan violent attacks calling for the murder of Israeli Jews through their Facebook pages.[1]

The suit raises important questions, including: When should the government initiate similar suits to impose criminal sanctions for targeted hate speech posted to Facebook? What constitute effective restrictions on social media that also balance society's need for robust dialogue and free communication, subject to limitations reflecting a need for order and respect among people?

There is a lack of resolution in the ongoing free speech discussion, particularly as it relates to social media. This is quickly becoming a critical focal point given the range, power and impact of the Internet. Social media is how and where contentious public issues are played out. Sometimes, the tone is ugly; numerous examples abound of posts that are racist, hurtful, and deeply insulting. Civil discourse is rare; anonymity enables hatred and calls for violence and harm to others, whether individuals or groups.

The essence of democracy is guaranteeing – and protecting – civil and political rights. Foremost among these rights is freedom of speech. Liberal, democratic governments recognize the right to free speech. The First Amendment

---

1 *Why 20,000 Israelis are Suing Facebook Over Palestinian Attacks*, PBS, Nov. 24, 2016, http://www.pbs.org/newshour/bb/why-20000-israelis-are-suing-facebook-over-palestinian-attacks/.

 | DOI 10.1163/9789004359826_016

of the U.S. Constitution guarantees the right to free speech. International conventions such as the International Covenant on Civil and Political Rights (ICCPR) similarly recognize it.[2]

Free speech is essential for vibrant, robust and rigorous debate, disagreement and contention. It reflects a healthy society, facilitating differences of opinion while respecting tolerance of diversity and creativity. Speech can make us uncomfortable, challenge us, and push us out of our comfort zones.

The right to free speech is not unlimited. The right is not sacrosanct. Democracies recognize that certain limits may – if not, must – be placed on these rights. U.S. law and jurisprudence recognize a difference between protected speech and unprotected speech, as discussed below.

The relationship between extremism, tolerance, and free speech is complex. Extremism in speech is not a new phenomenon; any effort to limit its scope and impact must be done with sensitivity and respect for otherwise guaranteed rights. However, extremist hate speech confronting – if not challenging – contemporary society is exacerbated both by the tone of the current political climate and the power, speed, and reach of the Internet.

Social networks facilitated by Facebook, Twitter, Google, and YouTube dramatically impact how the message of extremism is conveyed. One of the great challenges confronting democratic decision makers is responding to the Internet's facilitation of extremism while respecting individual and civil rights.

In other words, the challenge is to determine what degree of extremist Internet speech can be tolerated – in the context of freedom of speech – before determining that extremist speech poses a clear and present danger. Balancing is fraught with danger; the consequences of unjustified limitations of free speech are antithetical to a democracy. On the other hand, speech has the potential of harming. The adage "words kill" is neither amorphous nor abstract.

2 Limiting Internet Speech

The free speech analysis requires a determination whether the proposed restriction is content-based or content-neutral. The former refers to restrictions that apply to particular viewpoints, thereby suggesting the proposed restriction carries a heavy presumption that it violates the First Amendment.[3]

---

2 U.S. Const. Amend. I; International Covenant on Civil and Political Rights, United Nations, Treaty Series, vol. 999, page 171, http://www.ohchr.org/en/professionalinterest/pages/ccpr.aspx/.

3 *Burson v. Freeman*, 504 U.S. 191 (1992).

When addressing viewpoint-based restrictions, the Supreme Court applies the most stringent standard of judicial review, known as strict scrutiny, in evaluating its lawfulness. To survive strict scrutiny, the restriction must be necessary to achieve a compelling government purpose.[4] That means that it cannot be, among other things, over-inclusive, under-inclusive, or vague. This standard effectively places a heavy burden on the government to defend the restriction.

However, if the restriction is content-neutral, meaning that the concern is not with the speech itself but rather pertains to the details surrounding the speech, then the government is allowed to set certain parameters involving time, place, and manner.[5] Content-neutral restrictions on speech are reviewed under intermediate scrutiny rather than strict scrutiny because the speech is restricted solely in the manner in which the information is communicated rather than content itself.

In *United States v. O'Brien*, the Supreme Court established a four-part test to determine whether a content-neutral restriction on speech is constitutional: (1) Is the restriction within the constitutional power of government, (2) Does the restriction further an important or substantial governmental interest, (3) Is the governmental interest unrelated to the suppression of free expression, (4) Is the restriction narrowly tailored, meaning no greater than necessary.[6]

Subsequently, a fifth factor was added in *City of Ladue v. Gilleo*, inquiring whether the restriction leaves open ample opportunities of communication.[7] Finally, there is an exception to the content-based rule that requires an analysis of the value of the speech in question. Certain forms of speech, such as political speech, are thought to be at the very core of the First Amendment's protection, and therefore merit the greatest protection under the law.[8] The *O'Brien* framework thus helps to establish a framework for how discriminatory, intimidating, disapproving, antagonistic, or prejudicial attitudes expressed towards a disliked target group should be limited within the context of social media.

There are no "safe spaces" on the Internet. To engage on the Internet is to join a fray, oftentimes contentious, and sometimes violent in its language. Although the First Amendment protects vile and odious speech, balancing the free speech interests of the speaker with the content of the chosen platform,

4 *Adarand Constructors, Inc. v. Pena*, 515 U.S. 200 (1995).

5 *Watchtower Bible & Tract Soc'y of N.Y., Inc. v. Vill. of Stratton*, 536 U.S. 150, 175 (2002).

6 *United States v. O'Brien*, 391 U.S. 367, 382 (1968).

7 *City of Ladue v. Gilleo*, 512 U.S. 43 (1994).

8 *See generally: Buckley v. Valeo*, 424 U.S. 1 (1976).

safety, and privacy concerns continue to present an ongoing struggle in the Internet age.

The harm is hate speech on the Internet; speech that is distinct from offensive speech. The former must be limited; the latter, regardless of the discomfort it may cause, must be tolerated. The question, based on case law, is how to resolve the limit-tolerate dilemma. That is, the discussion must go beyond the "moral and social responsibility" and articulate legal contours.

The following standard is proposed for determining whether speech morphs into social media hate speech that can be limited: Social media speech cannot be limited through imposition of a bright line rule or an exacting formula. Postings must be assessed on a sliding scale taking into account multiple factors including magnitude, frequency, intent of the platform, and content of the post and platform.[9] The proposal is based on a suggested Internet-based re-articulation of the *Brandenburg* test. This recommendation minimizes government excess as it reflects sensitivity to the distinct nature of social media speech while simultaneously recognizing the harm posed by hate speech on the Internet.

Internet speech is different from traditional speech; that difference is particularly important because the future of social media remains unknown, and it would be erroneous to establish a bright line rule articulating when Internet speech should be limited. One of the dangers of an approach that does not tolerate flexibility is enforcement. It is counterproductive to dictate prosecution in accordance with a rule devoid of nuance and flexibility. It is, however, productive to recognize that the Internet's inherent fluidity and unique nature lends itself to a case-by-case approach to determine when limits need be imposed. Attempting to articulate a bright line rule – given the nature of Internet speech as analyzed by Cohen-Almagor[10] – invites government excess when not warranted.

3 Learning from the Rabin Assassination

Those who lived in Israel prior to the assassination of Prime Minister Yitzhak Rabin well recall the incessant, consistent and loud incitement articulated by

---

9 Contributed by Jonathan Vick, Assistant Director, Cyberhate Response, Anti-Defamation League. Mr. Vick's substantive contribution of pivotal factors to assess when limiting speech are described below.

10 Raphael Cohen-Almagor, Confronting the Internet's Dark Side: Moral and Social Responsibility on the Free Highway (2015).

rabbis and others. The unceasing nature of the hate speech directed at Rabin directly contributed to Yigal Amir's decision to assassinate Rabin. That is relevant for our purposes for it highlights – tragically – the consequences of unlimited, unrestrained, and unremitted speech.

Recurring threats are different from single occurrence threats that may not have the same inciting impact. It is for that reason that the proposal above is particularly focused on repetitive speech that suggests a pattern that is more likely to pose harm. Such a limiting paradigm is more aligned with a suitable method for applying *Brandenburg* to social media. While a one-time viable threat may also be limited; however, the threats that pose the greatest danger are those articulated consistently over time.

With consistency, the magnitude of the threat becomes more realistic, directly corresponding to increased frequency. Accordingly, patterns of hate speech stated on a regular basis warrant special attention and are one factor that must be assessed when determining if speech should be limited.

The context or venue in which Internet speech takes place is perhaps the most pivotal factor in assessing whether speech need be limited. Certain websites intentionally make their forum platform a safe haven for discriminatory hate speech.[11] These forums serve as a closed community in which like-minded individuals share hate speech posts that support their cause. A webpage dedicated to sharing views in an online forum has less far-reaching implication than posting similar hate speech on immediately disseminated social media pages like Twitter and Facebook. The latter social media platforms disseminate information almost instantaneously to a vast audience and inevitably have the impact to marginalize those targeted by the speech. Accordingly, the context of the chosen platform is directly linked to the far-reaching intent and magnitude of the speech.

Speech must be handled with sensitivity, intelligence, and honesty. Thus, in conjunction with *Brandenburg*,[12] it is appropriate to apply J.S. Mill's principle: when it is reasonable and feasible to assume that an act (of speech in that case) will cause harm to others, we should prevent it. If it is unclear whether speech will result in harm, that speech must be protected; otherwise over-reach is the inevitable and problematic result. These joint principles reinforce a case-by-case approach to determine appropriate limitations to Internet speech.

---

11 *See for example:* Stormfront.org, a neo-Nazi forum that predates the Internet, and is run by a former Klu Klux Klan Grand Dragon, David Duke. The White Supremacist group makes its online home at the stormfront.org website.

12 *Brandenburg v. Ohio*, 395 U.S. 444 (1969).

4 Exploration of Real World Examples

The transnational impact of social media is particularly pertinent when exploring the extent to which government should be allowed to limit Internet speech. Some democratic countries have legislated in the area of state responsibility, but the effectiveness of such legislation is potentially limited by national boundaries, absent the cooperation of other countries.[13] The essence of the problem is the legal difficulty democratic societies experience in addressing the problem of hate speech on the Internet. The argument of responsibility and the call for a sense of responsibility is compelling. It must, nevertheless, be buttressed by limits established by law that include enforcement mechanisms and punishment. Such limitations are necessary to combat hate speech posing danger to individuals and society alike.

In the U.S., the content-neutrality principle in the application of the First Amendment severely constrains government's ability to deal with the problem.[14] This is, then, a disturbing weakness that highlights the limits with which governments can counter – much less minimize – hate speech on the Internet. For example, Facebook's claim to be a content-free platform of communication is likely legally defensible, even though practically illogical. The narrow instance in which the government's ability to limit violent hate speech occurs when *there is a targeted and specific threat to an individual person or group.*

Although speech cannot be limited with a bright line rule, a substantial number of factors contribute to when speech could be limited. The principle articulated above is a useful starting point – when it is reasonable and feasible to assume that an act of Internet speech will cause harm to others, we should prevent it. Targeted hate speech that carries with it immediate harm (capability to carry out the violence), individualized harm (capability to assault the target), and capability to carry out the threat (actualized means of committing the violence), must be limited.

The public has been confronted with a number of significant free speech issues in the past few years; this essay examines four real world examples. In analyzing these examples, the point of inquiry is whether the test articulated by the Supreme Court in *Brandenburg* when applied to Internet speech sufficiently protects the speaker, the audience, the larger public and the intended

13 *See generally:* Raphael Cohen-Almagor, CONFRONTING THE INTERNET'S DARK SIDE: MORAL AND SOCIAL RESPONSIBILITY ON THE FREE HIGHWAY (2015) at 230 (discussion on State Responsibility); *See for example: Yahoo! Inc. v. La Ligue Contre Le Racisme et L'Antisemitisme,* 169 F.2d 1181 (N.D.Cal. 2001), *rev'd.,* 433 F. 3d 1199 (9th Cir.), *cert. den.* 547 U.S. 1163 (2006).

14 *See for example: R.A.V. v. City of St. Paul,* 505 U.S. 377 (1992).

target of the speech. Only one example below highlights the narrow instance where limitation of Internet speech would be appropriate.

4.1 *Ted Nugent's Antisemitic National Rifle Association Posting*

Ted Nugent's February 8, 2016 Facebook post (a share that had previously appeared on antisemitic websites) features Israeli flags on a collage of the faces of prominent Jewish Americans with the text, "So who is really behind gun control?" Mr. Nugent's controversial and antisemitic message drew national news coverage and criticism of Mr. Nugent, an outspoken advocate of gun-rights and the Second Amendment. The antisemitic graphic received praise by some groups, condemnation by others, and started an active online debate.[15]

The Anti-Defamation League (ADL)[16] called for removal of Nugent's post.[17] Although it is legitimate for the ADL, and other private actors generally, to call for removal of controversial viewpoints and build popular pressure to cause the NRA to distance itself publicly from Nugent's views, the same cannot be said for a government body mandating limitation of the speech.[18] This is not an instance in which the government could limit Internet speech. As antisemitic, or odious as Mr. Nugent's posting may be, it need not be removed from social media.[19]

4.2 *Inflammatory Sam Houston State University Student Tweet*

Consider the following September 2015 Twitter posting ("tweet") by Sam Houston State University ("SHSU") student Monica Foy. Her post was connected to the death of Harris County, Texas Sheriff's Deputy Darren Goforth, who was killed August 28, 2015 while pumping gas into his police car.

15 Brad Devereaux, *Ted Nugent replies "eat me" to critics of "anti-Semitic" gun control post*, MLive Media Group, February 13, 2016, http://www.mlive.com/news/index.ssf/2016/02/ted_nugents_anti-semitic_gun_c.html.

16 About the Anti-Defamation League, ADL, http://www.adl.org/about-adl/. According to their website, the ADL was founded in 1913 "to stop the defamation of the Jewish people and to secure justice and fair treatment to all".

17 ADL Calls on Ted Nugent to Remove Facebook Post Targeting Prominent Jews for Supporting Gun Control, ADL, February 8, 2016, https://www.adl.org/news/press-releases/adl-calls-on-ted-nugent-to-remove-facebook-post-targeting-prominent-jews-for.

18 For example, Oberlin College in Ohio was recently at the center of a social media controversy regarding Facebook postings made by one of its professors, Joy Karega. Karega posted a number of antisemitic statements on her Facebook page. Oberlin College is a private actor and the issue is not a question in which the government may intervene.

19 Nugent's response to the criticism can be found here: February 8, 2016, https://www.facebook.com/tednugent/posts/10153471495187297.

Ms. Foy tweeted, "I can't believe so many people care about a dead cop and NO ONE has thought to ask what he did to deserve it. He had creepy perv eyes...."[20]

Multiple news sources picked up the tweet and the ensuing backlash caused the tweet to go viral, despite Ms. Foy deleting it. Ms. Foy received threats, later issued an apology, and was also arrested on an outstanding warrant for a previous assault charge.

SHSU responded shortly after Ms. Foy's initial tweet, issuing the following statement: "SHSU has a strong Student Code of Conduct. The student's remarks will be evaluated to determine if the code was violated following standardized due process. The university has an ongoing commitment to taking actions that strengthen dialog and understanding between our students and the law enforcement community."[21] This response provoked additional controversy; SHSU was criticized for both contemplating limiting Ms. Foy's First Amendment rights and for not taking more aggressive action to limit the distasteful speech. The criticism highlighted the complexity of the free speech discussion – while some would argue Ms. Foy's post typified the "dark side"[22] Cohen-Almagor notes, others would suggest the post articulated a legitimate position in the context of an important public discussion regarding the relationship between law enforcement and the public. That discussion, as uncomfortable and controversial as it may be, is "front and center" in America and to that end, posts – even if "edgy" – need not be limited.

SHSU President Dana Hoyt issued a statement after "much time" examining the "careless remarks" of Ms. Foy; President Hoyt clarified Ms. Foy would not be punished for her remarks.[23] Hoyt stated, "A personal comment made on a private social media account, as offensive as it was, remains protected by the First Amendment. Offensive speech is still protected speech."[24] Hoyt went on to state, "Ms. Foy has issued an apology and will have to live with the consequences of her actions ... Our response maintains both our academic integrity and upholds the Constitution of the United States of America. Sometimes the

20 *Apologetic Sam Houston State Student Won't Get Punished by Sam for Tweet*, KBTX, Sept. 5, 2015, http://www.kbtx.com/home/headlines/Apologetic-Sam-Houston-State-Student-Wont-Get-Punished-by-Sam-for-Tweet-324742191.html.

21 *Id.*

22 Raphael Cohen-Almagor, CONFRONTING THE INTERNET'S DARK SIDE: MORAL AND SOCIAL RESPONSIBILITY ON THE FREE HIGHWAY (2015).

23 *Apologetic Sam Houston State Student Won't Get Punished by Sam for Tweet*, KBTX, Sept. 5, 2015, http://www.kbtx.com/home/headlines/Apologetic-Sam-Houston-State-Student-Wont-Get-Punished-by-Sam-for-Tweet-324742191.html.

24 *Id.*

right choice is not always the most popular decision."[25] In this instance, SHSU correctly determined Ms. Foy's speech can be considered offensive by some, but is ultimately harmless, and therefore should not be limited.

4.3 *Palestinian Terrorist Facebook Posts Encouraging Vehicle Run Over Attacks*

In late 2015, numerous Palestinian terrorist groups posted messages on social media encouraging Palestinians to commit car-ramming attacks intended to run over Jews. For example, on November 28, 2015, one Facebook post read: "Run away, my friend ... this is not your land. Resist, oh son of Jerusalem. Resist, oh son of the [West] Bank. Run over the Zionists." Another posting included an image and text that read: "Death of a Zionist officer and wounding of a soldier. Death as a martyr for the sake of Allah of Ibrahim Sakafi in Hebron [the perpetrator of the attack]. Run them over. The intifada continues." The image depicts a vehicle skidding over an Israeli flag and was posted the day after a vehicular attack.[26]

---

25 *Id.*

26 For more on what has been called the "car intifada" *See:* MEIR AMIT INTELLIGENCE AND TERRORISM INFORMATION CENTER, *Vehicular Attacks: A Lethal, Easily-Executed Type of Attack Most are carried out by lone operatives unaffiliated with terrorist organizations although sometimes inspired by them*, July 24, 2015, http://www.terrorism-info.org.il/Data/articles/Art_21041/E_133_16_830403212.pdf ; Itamar Marcus and Nan Jacques Zilberdik, *Palestinian song encourages more terror*, PALESTINIAN MEDIA WATCH, November 10, 2014, http://www.palwatch.org/main.aspx?fi=157&doc_id=13007; Elior Levy, *"Car intifada" cartoon campaign encourages vehicular attacks*, YNET NEWS, November 6, 2014, http://www.ynetnews.com/articles/0,7340,L-4588776,00.html. For examples of Palestinian incitement on Facebook and elsewhere *See Social Media as a Platform for Incitement – Part IV: Hashtag "Stab" on Twitter, Facebook*, Special Dispatch No. 6237, December 10, 2015, MEMRI, https://www.memri.org/reports/social-media-platform-incitement-part-iv-hashtag-stab-twitter-facebook; *Social Media as a Platform for Incitement – Part III: Posting Pictures of Small Children Wielding Knives as Praise, Encouragement for Terrorism*, Special Dispatch No. 6197, October 22, 2015, MEMRI, https://www.memri.org/reports/social-media-platform-incitement-%E2%80%93-part-iii-posting-pictures-small-children-wielding-knives; Ariel Ben Solomon, *Photos: Social media and Palestinian incitement during terror wave*, THE JERUSALEM POST, October 16, 2015. *See also:* Paul Alster, *"Stab the Zionist": Palestinian songs celebrate killing Jews*, FOXNEWS.COM, November 12, 2015, http://www.foxnews.com/world/2015/11/12/sick-hit-parade-palestinian-songs-celebrate-stabbing-jews.html ; *Israel takes on Facebook in battle against incitement*, YNET NEWS, July 21, 2016, http://www.ynetnews.com/articles/0,7340,L-4831483,00.html; *Israel Decries Facebook, YouTube Policy Allowing Anti-Jewish Incitement, Holocaust Denial on Pages*, 5 TOWNS JEWISH TIMES, February 15, 2016, http://5tjt.com/israel-decries-facebook-you

There are colorable arguments on both sides of the issue of whether these postings should be restricted. In the context of Professor Cohen-Almagor's argument regarding "social and moral responsibility,"[27] it appears that the postings violated standards of responsibility, however, it would be inappropriate to limit the free speech of the posters in accordance with *Brandenburg*. Unlike the posting with specific instructions on how to stab a Jew to death discussed below, this posting is more general and therefore less clear in its "how to" instructions. Although there is little doubt as to the intent of the posting and the fact that Palestinians did indeed commit "car ramming" terrorist attacks, limiting the post would be an overreaching attempt to limit free speech. The recommendation not to do so reflects a legal argument positing that the speakers do not pose a threat both to specific individuals and larger society. The irresponsibility, and lack of moral and social responsibility of the posters does not justify imposition of legal restrictions.

The counter-argument to this conclusion is that the speaker can inflict immediate harm by operating a motor vehicle (capability to carry out the violence), the harm is individualized (capability to assault the target walking down the street), and the capability to carry out the threat is readily accessible (actualized means of committing the violence with their car is realistic). Nevertheless, this generalized posting is not an instance that warrants limitation.

4.4 *Palestinian Terrorist Facebook Stabbing Attack Posts*

As briefly noted in the introduction, in October and November 2015, Palestinian terrorists issued a widespread call for stabbing attacks against Jewish citizens living in Israel. Consequently, in October 2015, twenty thousand Israelis joined a civil lawsuit filed in the Supreme Court for the State of New York by

---

tube-policy-allowing-anti-jewish-incitement-holocaust-denial-on-pages/; *Police arrest Jerusalem Arabs for online incitement*, ARUTZ SHEVA, December 18, 2016, http://www.israelnationalnews.com/News/News.aspx/221888; Yoel Domb, *Israel cracks down on incitement in east Jerusalem schools*, ARUTZ SHEVA, August 25, 2016, http://www.israelnationalnews.com/News/News.aspx/216932; EUROPEISRAËL NEWS, December 2015, http://static.europe-israel.org/wp-content/uploads/2015/12/violon-couteau.jpg; 5 TOWNS JEWISH TIMES, February 2016, http://5tjt.com/wp-content/uploads/2016/02/303135-thumb.jpg; Facebook page of Fatima Elharithi, October 16, 2015, https://www.facebook.com/photo.php?fbid=539967812833526&set=a.102314363265542.5470.100004609354819&type=3&theater.

27 Raphael Cohen-Almagor, CONFRONTING THE INTERNET'S DARK SIDE: MORAL AND SOCIAL RESPONSIBILITY ON THE FREE HIGHWAY (2015).

Shurat HaDin, an Israeli civil rights organization, against Facebook. The suit alleged that Facebook allowed Palestinian extremists to openly recruit and train terrorists to conduct violent attacks against Israeli Jews. Although the court dismissed the lawsuit in May 2017 on the grounds that Facebook is immune from prosecution under the Communications Decency Act,[28] the plaintiffs have vowed to appeal the court's dismissal of the lawsuit.[29]

An Israeli Ministry of Foreign Affairs official slammed Facebook and YouTube for rejecting repeated requests to automatically intercept content that could lead to assaults against Jews.[30] The official stressed the problematic nature both of recruitment on Facebook of many young people by radical Islamist groups and of "lone-wolf" Palestinian terrorists incited to kill Jews in Israel. One Facebook image and accompanying video purported to teach would-be Palestinian attackers "how to stab" Jews.[31] Detailed and violent photos posted to social media include step-by-step instructions for maximizing bodily damage against Jews.

This is a narrow instance where speech should be limited. The speech is targeted hate speech that carries with it each of the aforementioned criteria for limiting speech: immediate harm (capability to carry out the violence on identifiable target with growing momentum of attacks), individualized harm (capability to assault the target/neighbor/individual walking down the street), and capability to carry out the threat (actualized means of committing the violence with a common knife).

5 Conclusion

Swastikas spray-painted on the door of a Colorado elementary school[32] and on several college campuses.[33] A rally for the President-elect of the United States

28 47 U.S.C. §230.

29 *NY court drops suit against Facebook over Palestinian incitement*, THE TIMES OF ISRAEL, May 19, 2017.

30 Ruthie Blum, *Israel Decries Facebook, YouTube Policy Allowing Anti-Jewish Incitement, Holocaust Denial on Pages*, THE ALGEMEINER, February 15, 2016.

31 *See:* Palestinian Media Watch, December 9, 2015, https://www.youtube.com/watch?v=96NUN1VIq-A.

32 Anica Padilla and Michael Konopasek, *Swastikas painted on elementary school in Stapleton,* FOX 31 DENVER, November 20, 2016.

33 Josh Kaplan, *Swastikas are appearing at colleges across America – but how worried should we be?* THE TAB, December 5, 2016.

featuring a "Heil Hitler" salute.[34] A proposed registry for Muslims leading to unease and fear across communities.[35]

Benjamin Kuperman, a professor at Oberlin College, awoke to sounds of tapping outside his home to find a note behind his mezuzah (a small case that contains verses from the Torah, common for Jews to place on their door frames) that stated, "Gas Jews Die."[36] A similar scenario unfolded at Harvard University, where a professor recently received a postcard stating, "Juden raus!"[37] a phrase introduced by the Nazis that translates to mean "Jews out."

Take out the location and time stamp on the aforementioned examples and it is easy to see why many are comparing the rise of the alt-right in the U.S. to Nazi Germany decades ago. To some, these incidents are clear-cut examples of hate speech. To others, expressing the viewpoint of the so-called white nationalist movement is a First Amendment right that should be allowed – and celebrated – as free speech without censorship.

The growing division between these schools of thought brings up a simple question with a complicated answer: How much intolerance should be tolerated?

Some may argue the issue was settled long ago in *Brandenburg v. Ohio*, the landmark U.S. Supreme Court ruling from 1969 when the Court reversed the conviction of a Ku Klux Klan leader who had advocated violence. Clarence Brandenburg was charged and convicted for advocating violence under Ohio's criminal syndicalism statute in 1964 for speeches he made.

At one rally, he stated "Personally, I believe the n – should be returned to Africa, the Jew returned to Israel." He also commented – as several Klan members stood by with firearms – "We're not a revengent organization, but if our President, our Congress, our Supreme Court, continues to suppress the white, Caucasian race, it's possible that there might have to be some revengeance taken."

Brandenburg appealed his conviction to the U.S. Supreme Court, claiming Ohio's statute violated his First Amendment rights under the U.S. Constitution. The court sided with him, issuing what is still considered today to be its most speech-protective holding. The ruling created a litmus test citing three

34 Jessica Roy, *Neo-Nazi "alt-right" crowd cheers the president-elect with "Hail Trump"*, LOS ANGELES TIMES, November 21, 2016.

35 Dave Perry, *Trump sparks fear for Colorado Muslims, everyone,* AURORA SENTINEL, November 29, 2016.

36 *Jewish Oberlin professor's house vandalized, note says "Gas Die Jew,"* JTA, November. 20, 2016.

37 Caleb Downs, *Postcard with anti-Semitic slurs sent to University of Texas law professor at Harvard,* THE DALLAS MORNING NEWS, November 22, 2016.

factors when speech can be prohibited: 1) if the speech promotes imminent harm, 2) there is a high likelihood the speech will result in listeners participating in illegal action and 3) the speaker intended to incite others to participate in illegality.[38]

The task of drawing the line in determining when speech incites others to behave is enormously complex.

The 1969 ruling came well before the digital age. We live in a time where clicks and shares spread hate and false information instantaneously across the Internet.

Given the tone and tenor in society following the election of Donald Trump, I believe it is time to revisit limits on free speech.

The challenge is to determine what degree of extremist Internet speech can be tolerated – in the context of freedom of speech – before determining that extremist speech poses a clear and present danger. Balancing is essential; the consequences of unjustified limitations of free speech are antithetical to a democracy. On the other hand, speech has the potential for harming. The adage "words kill" is neither amorphous nor abstract.

Speech must be handled with sensitivity, intelligence, and honesty. When reasonable to assume speech will cause harm to others, we should prevent it. If unclear whether speech will result in harm, it must be protected; otherwise overreach is the inevitable and problematic result.

Brandenburg must be understood to not only protect the speaker's rights, but to also ensure protection of potential targets. As has been made dramatically clear in the past weeks there is potential danger to minority groups. They are deserving of our protection. We are living in a time when reports of hate are surfacing at an alarming rate.

The First Amendment limitations primarily address the government-citizen axis of speech constraint. Social media companies like Facebook and Twitter are private enterprises, and accordingly fall on the citizen-citizen axis.[39] It is for that reason that adoption of legal limits on free speech in social media is essential. In proposing establishment of legal limits on social media, the primary concern is balancing victim and speaker rights. Needless to say, the implications of recommending the imposition of restrictions on free speech in the social media age are problematic and troublesome.

In narrow circumstances, the *duty* to legally protect victims of hate speech outweighs the privilege of freedom of speech otherwise granted to those who engage in social media.

---

38 *Brandenburg v. Ohio*, 395 U.S. 444, 447–448 (1969).

39 *See: Citizens United v. Federal Election Commission*, 558 U.S. 310 (2010).

Combating Incitement to Violence on the Internet through Service Provider Action

David Matas

Simply to get internet access to virtually any internet platform, we click an icon acknowledging that we agree to the terms of service of the internet provider. If we bother to look, we can see that internet providers prohibit incitement to violence on the internet.

We can also see that providers have complaints procedures and that they commit in principle to denying service to those who violate their terms of service. Indeed, when we click on the tab "I agree," that is the agreement – respect the terms of service or lose access to the service.

If that is all we knew, we might think that there is no problem. We might think that the incitement to violence which we see on the internet is just the result of lag time between posting of incitement and the resolution of the complaints procedures.

Yet that thought is an assumption. Only through monitoring and analysis, by delving into the figures, can we see whether the systems in place for prohibiting the use of the internet for incitement to violence are working.

It does not take much investigation to realize that the problem with the internet in this area, in a nutshell, is that incitement to violence is prohibited everywhere in theory, but very little in practice. The system in place is not working.

Moreover, this is not a legal or governmental or police system that is failing. This is the system the internet providers have set up for themselves. Unless we look at the functioning of the system, we would miss this reality.

We should be able, in principle, to consider complaints to internet providers and what is done with them. How many complaints are there? What happens to them? Are they accepted or rejected? Does acceptance mean removing the content, blocking the person who posted or denying access to the source of the materials? Who are the readers of the material? Does the result vary by country? By type of content? If either accepted or rejected, what are the reasons for the decision? What are the lag times between complaints and decisions? How do various internet providers differ in answers to these questions?

Those instances of incitement to violence which are seen by the greatest number, those which are likely to cause the most harm, are the items which will be complained about most often. They are both the most important to consider and, because of the complaints they generate, the easiest to determine.

 | DOI 10.1163/9789004359826_017

There is no good reason why internet providers should prohibit use of their service to incite violence and then allow it to happen. When internet providers prohibit use of their service to incite violence and then allow it to happen, something is amiss. But what?

That question is not easy to answer because of the opacity of internet providers. Internet providers, who, in theory, tout openness as the very basis of their business, are far from open about the abuse of their services.

Internet providers produce reports on the workings of their complaints procedures. Some of these reports are boldly called transparency reports. Yet, these reports are not all that transparent.

The internet providers do not have a problem collecting data about abuse. The providers have the data through the complaints procedure. But they do not disclose what they have. Companies that advocate openness and need openness for the effective functioning of their businesses are far from open about how they deal with incitement to violence. In what follows, I use Google's policies and practices as an example.

1 Google

Google, in a variety of ways, prohibits use of its products to incite violence. Under the heading "Hate Speech," its User Content and Conduct Policy states:

> ... we don't support content that promotes or condones violence against individuals or groups based on race or ethnic origin, religion, disability, gender, age, nationality, veteran status, or sexual orientation/gender identity, or whose primary purpose is ... if the primary purpose is to attack a protected group, the content crosses the line.[1]

Under the heading "Harassment, Bullying, and Threats," the policy states:

> Do not engage in ... threatening behavior, and do not incite others to engage in these activities. Anyone using our Services ... to threaten someone with serious harm ... may have the offending content removed or be permanently banned from using the Services. In emergency situations, we may escalate imminent threats of serious harm to law enforcement.[2]

---

1 Google, *User Content and Conduct Policy*, https://www.google.com/intl/en-US/+/policy/content.html.

2 *Id.*

Under the heading "Violence," the policy states:

> Do not distribute depictions of graphic or gratuitous violence.[3]

Under the heading "Illegal Activities," the policy states:

> Do not use our Services to engage in illegal activities or to promote activities that are dangerous and illegal, such as terrorism ....[4]

Specific Google products have their own similar policies. YouTube Community Guidelines, for instance, provide:

> Violent or graphic content
> Don't encourage others to commit specific acts of violence.[5]

Under the heading "Hateful content," as well as under the heading "Threats," the very policy Google quoted earlier under the headings "Hate Speech" and "Harassment, Bullying, and Threats" appears.[6]

YouTube further states in its "Violent or Graphic Content Policy"

> Content Related to Terrorism
> YouTube strictly prohibits content intended to recruit for terrorist organizations, incite violence, celebrate terrorist attacks or otherwise promote acts of terrorism. We also do not permit foreign terrorist organizations to use YouTube.[7]

Google's User Content and Conduct Policy apply to Google+, Blogger, Hangouts, Google Photos, Spaces and YouTube but not to Gmail. The Gmail Program Policies state, instead,

> Harassment
> Don't use Gmail to ... threaten others. Anyone found to be using Gmail for these purposes may have their account disabled.

---

3 *Id.*

4 *Id.*

5 Youtube, *Community Guidelines*, https://www.youtube.com/yt/policyandsafety/community guidelines.html.

6 *Id.*

7 *Id.*

> Illegal Activity
> Keep it legal. Don't use Gmail to promote, organize, or engage in unlawful activities.[8]

How many complaints does Google receive for violation of its policies against incitement to violence, threats and depiction of violence? How long does Google take to decide on the complaints? How many of the complaints are accepted and how many rejected? What is the breakdown of this information by country? What are the reasons for the decisions?

Google produces what it calls a Transparency Report on internet complaints, across all products. The report provides figures on requests from courts and government agencies to remove content such as blog posts, YouTube videos or search results. Private requests are not reported.[9]

The report gives examples which themselves are incomplete; in addition, they do not give an overall picture. For instance, the report provides this for Switzerland for the request period July to December 2015.

> Request: We received a request from the Swiss Attorney General to remove a film about the Syrian Revolution from YouTube because it allegedly supports 'a prohibited organization in its criminal activities through the use of propaganda (Art. 2 of the Fed Act)'.
> Outcome: We did not remove the videos.[10]

The request refers to a film. The outcome refers to videos. Was there one video or several? Why did Google not remove the film/videos? As noted, their policy is not to allow illegal content. Did Google disagree with the Swiss Attorney General about the legality of the film/videos under Swiss law? On its face, the decision is mysterious. Moreover, from what little Google tells about the film/videos, it would seem to violate its policies about incitement to violence and terrorism, even if legal. Did it not? If not, why not?

---

8 *Gmail Program Policies*, https://www.google.com/gmail/about/policy/.

9 Google, *Transparency Report*, https://www.google.com/transparencyreport/removals/government/?hl=en.

10 Google, *Transparency Report: Explore Requests- Switzerland, July to December 2015*, https://www.google.com/transparencyreport/removals/government/notes/?hl=en#authority=CH&period=Y2015H2.

Here is another example from the request period July to December 2014.

> Request: We received a request from Roscomnadzor to remove a Blogger blog post discussing jihad in Russia's North Caucasus regions.
> Outcome: We removed the content from blogger.ru.[11]

What was it about the discussion that justified the content removal? Which of the various policies on violence did the content violate? Why was the content removed but the user not barred from using the service?

The Transparency Report provides a breakdown by category by time period, category and country but only for the most recent period reported. For France, for instance, for the period July to December 2015 there were 3 government or court violence removal requests. The action on these requests is not reported.[12]

In theory, one could go through every country report in the Transparency Report Google produces to get an aggregate figure for violence requests. But why cannot Google do that for us? What is also missing is what happens to the complaints, how long it takes to deal with them, what is the Google product which is the basis of the complaint and what are the numbers of private complaints.

Simply getting to the place on the website that gives us these figures is not simple. It means going first to the Transparency Report, then clicking on "Government requests to remove content," then, in the section titled "Explore Requests from July to December 2015," clicking on the phrase "See more requests," then, in the "Explore Requests" section, choosing a particular country, and then, under the round flag-like symbol of the country, clicking on the name of the country. Since there is no indication at any point that a particular link leads to the data, finding the data means, for first time users, clicking everything in sight till the data pops up.

Google reports that its compliance rate for requests from French government agencies or law enforcement during the period was 59% and that its compliance rate for requests which include a court order was 81%. It seems odd that Google would be ignoring 29% of requests which included a court order. Google explains it this way:

11 Google, *Transparency Report: Explore Requests- Russia, July to December 2014*, https://www.google.com/transparencyreport/removals/government/notes/?hl=en#authority=RU&period=Y2014H2.

12 Google, *Transparency Report: France*, https://www.google.com/transparencyreport/removals/government/FR/?hl=en.

> Note that frequently court orders included with requests do not compel Google to take any action. Rather, they often result from a dispute with a third party and are submitted by the requesting user as evidence to support their claim that we should remove the content.[13]

Complainants are given across all requests. There is not a specific figure for violence compliance requests.

The Transparency Report sub-component for Germany states, without a time period indicated:

> We receive lists of URLs from BPjM (BPjM Modul), a federal government youth protection agency in Germany, for sites that contain content that violates German youth protection law, like content touting … extreme violence …, and we may remove those search results from google.de.[14]

The statement refers to violation of a local law rather than violation of a global standard prohibiting use of its products to incite violence. The statement refers to search results only, and not to YouTube, Blogger or other Google products. The statement refers also only to removing results from google.de and not all Google search sites. The statement says that Google "may remove" the results, not that they have removed the results or will remove the results. Nor do they indicate under what circumstances they would or would not remove those results from google.de.

It is not clear what other Google products like YouTube or Blogger do with potentially offending URLs from the federal government youth protection agency. Is there removal? What is removed? Is it content emanating from Germany? Is it content going into Germany? Is it only content that both emanates from and goes into Germany, so that content emanating from outside of Germany and going into Germany, as well as content emanating from Germany and going outside Germany is not removed? Or, as with the search engine itself, is it just the result of the search on YouTube, Blogger and so on, that is blocked, the content all the while remaining?

The phrase "removal requests" might seem to indicate that we are not dealing with the blocking of searches, since blocking a search result does not remove anything from the internet. It just prevents access through the Google search engine to the items blocked. However, as one can see, the Google Transparency

13 *Id.*

14 Google, *Transparency Report: Germany,* https://www.google.com/transparencyreport/removals/government/DE/?hl=en.

Report uses the term "removal" to refer to blocking, removing the results from the search engine.

The Google search engine does more than just search. It also provides autocomplete, a service which expands the requested search to include terms commonly used. But, regrettably, terms commonly used may incite violence. There are no statistics and there is no reporting on autocomplete in the Transparency Report.

Google cannot take down all incitement to violence on the internet. When it comes to search results, omitting specific results, and blocking access to them via Google, blocking is the best it can do, although it certainly could block globally rather than country by country. When it comes to its own products, it can remove the offending content entirely and not just block access to it from particular countries. But does it?

The Transparency Report states:

> Governments ask us to remove or review content for many different reasons. … The laws surrounding these issues vary by country.[15]

Laws and the content of incitement to violence may vary from country to country. The form of incitement may vary over time and place. But the terms of service are uniform globally.

Addressing incitement to violence country by country depending on what the local laws are not only runs contrary to the global nature of the terms of service; it also is more resource intensive than a global approach. Making determinations country by country means setting up country teams for every country to determine the applicability of local laws.

While saving Google money is not a concern I have, the fact that Google has chosen a means of implementing its incitement to violence policy that is resource intensive means that it is less likely to be done well. An expensive remedy is less likely to be implemented effectively than an inexpensive remedy.

How big are these country teams? Where are they located? What is their expertise? What is their budget? Do the country teams have staff dedicated only to incitement to violence, or are they doing everything? These are all questions unanswered by the Transparency Report.

The reference to local laws in the Transparency Report, the suggestion of variation from one country to the next, as well as a reference to government

15 Google, *Transparency Report,* https://www.google.com/transparencyreport/removals/government/?hl=en.

complaints only leads one to wonder whether Google has an operational concept of incitement to violence.

Are the Google terms of service on incitement to violence an illusion, giving the impression that incitement to violence is prohibited when in fact it is not? Is the prohibition of incitement to violence in the terms of service a cosmetic facade without any reality behind it? Only the release of information which Google has but does not provide would allow us to answer those questions.

This analysis may seem that I am being hard on Google. Yet, when it comes to transparency, compared to other internet providers, Google is a leader.

I have also, for the purpose of this presentation, looked at the transparency reports for Facebook, Twitter and Microsoft. The detail in the reports of others providers pales in comparison to what Google produces. I would not suggest that the manner in which Google presents its data should be emulated. But at least it should be commended for trying to come to grips, however feebly, with the issue of transparency in this area, which is more than can be said of some other internet providers.

2 Free Speech

While the individual transparency reports have their specific features, one common feature is the focus on government complaints. Although this is just a reporting restriction, it raises the question whether this is also a policy restriction.

Are providers, when it comes to violation of their terms of service, acting on government complaints only? Do they take government complaints more seriously than private complaints? Is the time lag shorter in dealing with government complaints than in dealing with private complaints?

This concern is not just a worry about downplaying of civil society, not just an objection to possible favouritism to Big Brother. The concern relates to content.

International and constitutional law protections for free speech typically apply to governments and not the private sector. Governments and legislatures must protect free speech. Private businesses are typically not subject to any such restriction. The right to freedom of expression does not impose on businesses an obligation to offer to the public the platforms the businesses provide without regard to the content members of the public wish to express.

In some countries the posting of content inciting to violence may prompt court action or legislation which would later allow for court action. Yet, ultimately, that sort of effort is indirect and raises, unnecessarily, the issue of the balance between the right to freedom of expression and the right to be free from incitement to violence.

Governments and legislatures may be constrained in what they can do about incitement to violence because of the duty to respect the right to free speech. For governments and legislatures, the right to free speech and the right to freedom from incitement to violence must be balanced against each other.

There is typically no similar externally imposed balancing requirement for private businesses, including internet providers. Internet providers may self-impose this balancing as part of their terms of service. But the fact remains that they have much greater latitude to block or remove incitement to violence from their sites than law enforcement agencies would have.

The internet providers, by reporting only on government requests for incitement to violence removal and blocking, may be signalling an artificial restriction on blocking and removing of this content. Internet providers may be limiting themselves only to what governments can do, when, legally, they do not have to be so limited. Have they restricted themselves in this way?

The focus on government requests can lead both to too much restriction and too little. Governments that comply with the requirement to respect freedom of speech will filter their requests through this requirement. Governments that do not respect freedom of speech will seek to expand their censorship beyond their reach through requests to internet providers. Giving priority to government requests may mean giving priority to requests for censorship of criticism of repressive governments.

Internet providers may focus on government requests to save money, since governments screen complaints before they pass them on. Internet providers, by a focus on government requests, offload screening costs onto governments.

Addressing incitement to violence is not an expertise that comes inherently with the businesses that Google has developed. For Google to rely on government and court edicts is a shortcut, avoiding the need for Google to have to make judgments it has no necessary skill in making.

Internet providers may focus on government requests in order to minimize the threat of legal action. Legal remedies for incitement to violence, in some countries or for some remedies, can be initiated only by governments or with government approval. Even where individuals can bring internet providers to court, governments have deeper pockets and specialized institutions and capacity to do so.

This offloading of costs or avoidance of litigation, if that is all that it is, is not content free, since governments take into account, indeed must take into account, freedom of speech constraints that do not apply to the private sector.

Whether internet providers, through a focus on government requests, intend freedom of speech constraints that legally do not apply to them or are an unintended consequence of that focus, the result is the same.

3 Shadow Reporting

The woeful state of internet provider reporting has led to a mimicking device, asking the public to report incitement to violence on the internet not just to internet providers but also to web sites set up for that purpose.

The Global Forum for Combating Antisemitism, a periodic global gathering of NGOs, academics and government representatives dedicated to combating antisemitism, hosted by the Ministry of Foreign Affair of the Government of Israel, led to the establishment of one of these websites. The Forum in 2009 was divided into working groups.[16] The 2009 Working Group report, its first, outlined a number of challenges to combating online antisemitism. The first was to address the fact that:

> We have a lack of metrics on:
> a. The number of problem items in specific platforms e.g. reported groups in Facebook, reported Videos on YouTube
> b. The number of items resolved on specific platforms e.g. groups shut down, videos removed, complaints reviewed or dismissed ...
> d. The time delay between something being reported and action being taken in a specific platform.[17]

The 2013 Working Group meeting recommended the creation of a global database of antisemitic material. In response, the Australia-based Online Hate Prevention Institute, whose head is Working Group co-chair Andre Oboler, developed and launched the FightAgainstHate.com reporting tool in December 2014. The public were invited to report online hate speech to this online tool.

16 From then, Andre Oboler and I have been and remain co-chairs of the Working Group on Antisemitism on the Internet and in the Media.

17 Andre Oboler and David Matas, *Report of the Online Antisemitism Working Group*, January 31, 2010, http://www.zionismontheweb.org/Global_Forum_2009_Online_Antisemitism_Working_Group_Report.pdf.

In January 2016, the Global Forum released a report of data about Facebook, Twitter and YouTube compiled from reports to this tool, under the title "Measuring the Hate: The State of Antisemitism in Social Media."[18] The author of the report is Andre Oboler.

The authors of a UNESCO (United Nations Educational Scientific and Cultural Organization) publication released June 2015 wrote:

> Various organizations that have combatted hate speech in other forms or have defended the rights of specific groups in the past have found themselves playing an increasingly important role online. … Organizations like … the Australian-based Online Hate Prevention Institute … have become increasingly invested in combating online hate speech by putting pressure on internet intermediaries to act more strongly against online hate speech, and by raising awareness among users. …
>
> A second type of initiative promoted by some organizations is collecting complaints from users about specific types of content. This activity is particularly interesting when considered in relation to the internet intermediaries' processes of resolving cases of hate speech. While some companies have begun to publish public transparency reports listing requests that governments make for data, information, and content to be disclosed or removed, they have not released information about requests from individual users. When individuals flag content as inappropriate, they may be notified about the processing status of their complaints, but this process remains largely hidden to other users and organizations. This has the result of limiting the possibility of developing a broader understanding of what speech individuals deem to be offensive, inappropriate, insulting, or hateful. Examples of initiatives crowdsourcing requests to take action against specific types of messages include … the Online Hate Prevention Institute's Fight Against Hate. These initiatives serve as innovative tools for keeping track of hate speech across social networks and how different companies regulate it.[19]

18 Andre Oboler, *Measuring the Hate: The State of Antisemitism in Social Media*, 2016, https://www.scribd.com/doc/296756972/Measuring-the-Hate-The-State-of-Antisemitism-in-Social-Media.

19 Gargliardone I, Gal D, Alves T, Martinez G, *Countering Online Hate Speech*, June 20, 2015; Rachel Pollack Ichou (Ed), *World Trends in Freedom of Expression and Media Development: Special Digital Focus 2015*, UNESCO, November 2, 2015, http://unesdoc.unesco.org/images/0023/002349/234933e.pdf.

The Forum/Institute report has data streams that the internet providers could easily have compiled from the complaints they receive, but do not provide. There are three immediately obvious differences between internet provider transparency reports and the Forum/ Institute Report. One is that the Forum/ Institute Report gives us numbers for private complaints.

The second difference is that it gives us numbers on antisemitism. Beyond that, the antisemitism is broken down into four categories – promoting violence, Holocaust denial, Israel-related, and traditional. Here, promoting violence is a subset of antisemitism and not a head category of its own.

The third difference is that the Report tracks identified items over time, telling the reader whether, in aggregate, the items are removed and how long the removal takes. The report tells the reader whether, in aggregate, the identified items were taken down by June 11, 3 months after the items had been identified by the public, by August 7, 5 months after, and by January 25, 2016, 10 months after, or if the items remained online.

Following the Global Forum in May 2015, Facebook, YouTube and Twitter were each offered, in exchange for an undertaking to review them, the list of addresses to content on their platform that had been included in a draft of the Forum/Institute report. Twitter and YouTube agreed and were provided the list.

The combination in the Forum/Institute report of platforms, categories and delays means that there can be comparisons amongst all three. We can see which platform is more likely to remove incitement to violence and which platform addresses incitement to violence more quickly.

There are four striking features of the Forum/Institute report. One is the significant volume of incitement to violence on the internet. This may be obvious from just by a cursory glance at what is posted on the internet. Yet, a tabulation of numbers makes the point forcefully. This significant volume is apparent despite the limitations of the report, that it is based on voluntary identification by individuals who knew about the FightAgainstHate.com reporting tool at the time when reports were being requested.

The report analyzes 2,024 postings identified by the public to the website in January and February 2015. 115 of these postings, or 5%, promoted violence against Jews. The volume of incitement to violence on the internet that the Forum/Institute Report discloses shows that the lack of detail in internet provider transparency reports is masking a big problem. If voluntary reporting for two months identified 115 postings of incitement to violence against Jews, presumably the postings of incitement to violence generally would be much larger. Underneath the bland, vague over-generalized data the internet providers report is a seething pit of incitement to violence.

A second striking feature of the Forum/Institute Report is the consistency of its methodology across platforms. Since the Institute uses the same categories and measurements for Twitter, Facebook, and Google alike, it is possible to compare platforms. The differences in methodology of the internet provider transparency reports makes difficult the sort of comparisons in which the Institute Report is able to engage.

A third feature of the Institute Report is the contrast between the Institute that produced the report and the internet providers behind the platforms. The Institute is a shoestring NGO with meagre funding and staff. The internet providers are billion dollar enterprises. Yet, the Institute, with its minuscule size and resources and voluntary reporting only, was able to produce a far more detailed and informative report than any of the behemoth platforms.

A fourth feature is the absence of any correlation between the quality of reporting and the effectiveness in enforcing terms of service. Of the internet providers canvassed, Facebook is the worst in terms of reporting details, but the best in terms of removing incitement to violence content from its platform.

It would be wrong, nonetheless, to draw from this absence of correlation the conclusion that detailed reporting would not be an effective tool in combating antisemitism. The better existing reports are still so far off the mark that the true value of detailed reporting has yet to be tested.

Although the Global Forum of May 2015 did not have the final Forum/Institute report, they did have a draft. The recommendations of the Forum included that internet providers

> post on their websites
> (a) hate speech search results,
> (b) decisions and reasons on complaints, without identifying the complainants, both those accepted and those rejected, and
> (c) a running total for complaints of the numbers, categories, dispositions and average time between complaints and dispositions… make their internal data bases available to concerned NGOs for the purpose of analysis of the complaints process and their response …[20]

The Forum meets only periodically and is focused specifically on antisemitism. Human Rights Voices should take advantage of its continuity of operations and its wider scope to advocate actively for the implementation of a variation of

20 The Action Plan for Combating Antisemitism 2015 and Beyond and Final Statements, May 14, 2015, http://mfa.gov.il/MFA/AboutTheMinistry/Conferences-Seminars/GFCA2013/Documents/GFCA2015Booklet.pdf.

the Forum recommendations addressing the measurement of incitement to violence on the internet.

4 Suggestions

The context for combatting incitement to terrorism has shifted because, for terrorist leadership, the balance between incitement and action has shifted. Incitement used to be a justification for action and recruitment to prepare for action. Today it is a call to action.

Terrorism before was perpetrated by professional terrorists and trained recruits. Now it is crowdsourced.

Incitement has been given priority by terrorists as a tactic for spreading terrorism. Correspondingly, a focus on combating incitement to terrorism has to be given a priority in the fight against terrorism.

There is a tool box for combating incitement to terrorism. These tools include:

(1) monitoring and reporting on the efforts of internet providers to enforce their terms of service which prohibit incitement to violence;
(2) engaging internet providers to improve their efforts to report on and to enforce their terms of service which prohibit incitement to violence;
(3) engaging, either through private sector or government efforts, in direct denial of internet service to terrorism inciters;
(4) using civil law against terrorist inciters and their enablers and by so doing imposing a financial cost to incitement and its complicity;
(5) as part of the civil law effort against inciters, invoking the remedies of human rights commissions and tribunals, where they exist and are accessible for this purpose;
(6) enhancing enforcement of the current criminal law against inciters;
(7) strengthening, through amending legislation, the criminal law directed against incitement;
(8) relying on relevant doctrines of the international law of war to promote and justify specific measures to combat terrorist incitement in situations of armed conflict;
(9) giving priority to the combat against incitement to terrorism as a means of conduct of armed conflict with terrorist entities;
(10) relying on relevant international law doctrines applicable to peacetime to combat terrorist incitement in situations where the international law of war is not engaged;

(11) engaging the international law debate on the definition of terrorism so that terrorism directed against Jews or Israel is not accepted as an exception to the general international law prohibition against terrorism and incitement to terrorism;
(12) in order to counteract the incitement, engaging in outreach to communities which inciters have targeted.

The battle against terrorism can usefully draw on a variety of backgrounds and experiences. Individuals, governments and NGOs committed to combating terrorism need to become more aware of the range of options open to them.

Police and Incitement to Terrorism: The Challenge of Countering Violent Narratives

Robert R. Friedmann

The role of police in handling incitement to terrorism is rather limited and mostly ineffective. This is particularly sobering given that a large portion of terrorist activities are carried out by "inspired" individuals who are not necessarily sent by those who initiate terrorist acts but are rather followers of an ideology to which they have chosen to adhere, the source of which can be found in strategically targeted incitement.

Police typically resort to *reactive measures* that range from intelligence gathering to arrest that may or may not lead to filing charges. Intelligence includes various modes of information gathering (subject to the laws of the country), active surveillance and, at times, active disruption of a planned act in order to prevent it. In the U.S., the majority of the law enforcement agencies do not deal with incitement at all. Only large county, city, state, and particularly federal agencies have some sort of homeland security and intelligence apparatus. Information sharing at that level is usually done in cooperation with and under the guidance of federal law enforcement agencies, particularly the FBI. Intelligence agencies share relevant information worldwide (more with some countries, less with others) but it is important to add that most of these efforts are directed at collecting information on looming operations and attacks and almost none focus on the incitement that breeds, accompanies, and justifies such attacks.

Some police efforts are directed at employing *proactive measures*. The National Institute of Justice (NIJ), the Police Executive Research Forum (PERF), Duke University and the University of North Carolina released a report with a set of recommendations to use principles of community policing to prevent violent extremism.[1] One recent effort by the US National Counterterrorism

1 Schanzer, David et al. THE CHALLENGE AND PROMISE OF USING COMMUNITY POLICING STRATEGIES TO PREVENT VIOLENT EXTREMISM: A CALL FOR COMMUNITY PARTNERSHIPS WITH LAW ENFORCEMENT TO ENHANCE PUBLIC SAFETY. Triangle Center on Terrorism and Homeland Security Sanford School of Public Policy, Duke University (2016); Miller, Elizabeth et al. PROMISING PRACTICES FOR USING COMMUNITY POLICING TO PREVENT VIOLENT EXTREMISM: HOW TO CREATE AND IMPLEMENT A COMMUNITY OUTREACH

 | DOI 10.1163/9789004359826_018

Center (NCTC) focuses on attempts to counter violent extremism (CVE).[2] NCTC claims to "engage community awareness efforts across the United States, with the goal of giving communities the information and the tools they need to identify extremism in their midst and do something about it before it manifests itself in violence."[3]

The PERF and Duke reports adopted the principles of community policing to cope with incitement. Community policing (emerging in the mid-1980s) is based on a proactive approach (in addition to rather than instead of the reactive approach), on partnership building and on the public health model that is aimed at curbing the epidemiology of crime (in this case terrorism) by focusing on causal conditions, that are conducive to crime, and offering pertinent solutions.[4] The PERF and Duke guiding philosophy is based on community outreach, treating the community as a whole, making outreach transparent yet devoid of an intelligence aim, and focusing on public safety and quality of life issues. It aims to develop partnerships with local agencies including governments, NGOs, the private sector, professional associations, civic associations and academia.

Outreach should then be followed with an assessment and intervention plan focusing on diversion to non-criminal programs, assessing impact on public safety, formalizing plans with stakeholders, considering legal restrictions, and doing so with police involvement but not as leaders. In other words, proactive law enforcement is no longer police-centered but community-centered.

For police to establish community relationships they have to wear uniforms, be persistent, identify needs and deliver services accordingly, be willing to learn from the community, partner with leaders and produce relevant material in multiple languages. This has to be done while paying attention to, understanding and overcoming barriers – namely, understanding mistrust and addressing the needs of the community. These relationships have to be sustained over the long term by maintaining consistent contacts, following through on service delivery and establishing a succession plan for officers and community contacts.

PROGRAM. Police Executive Research Forum, Triangle Center on Terrorism and Homeland Security (2016).

2 Rasmussen, Nicholas J, Countering Violent Islamist Extremism: The Urgent Threat of Foreign Fighters and Homegrown Terror, Hearing before the House Committee on Homeland Security, February 11, 2015, https://www.nctc.gov/docs/Countering_Violent_Islamist_Extremism.pdf.

3 *Id.*

4 *See:* Robert R. Friedmann, COMMUNITY POLICING: COMPARATIVE PERSPECTIVES AND PROSPECTS. New York: St. Martin's Press (1992).

Herein also lies the dual challenge for policing incitement. First, very little of overall police operations is focusing on incitement. With public order, traffic, investigations, special events and the routine activities of police, not much attention is paid to incitement. There is no immediate hard data on police handling of incitement cases because such reports are not included in Part 1 and Part 2 crimes that police agencies have to report to the FBI.[5] It is fair however to assess that police agencies are handling a handful of cases of incitement and those will be forwarded to prosecution only in very rare cases where prosecutors believe they have a winnable case. Second, community policing advocacy sounds sensible and convincing and it is highly recommended as a strategy. This is particularly true given the dearth of any alternative. However, the drawback is the lack of wide-range implementation across large, mid-size and small departments. It is the exact same criticism that was leveled at community policing in its emergent days during the late 1980s.[6] Even if widely and successfully implemented, it is a long-term process not likely to yield desirable results in the near future. The missing link in proactive policing against incitement and violent extremism is the glaring dearth of suggested metrics – not to mention hard data – to measure and support any claims of success.

A related issue has to do with the clear lack of an agreeable and accepted definition of terrorism and along with it a definition of incitement. From a legal viewpoint, no protection under the First Amendment will be granted if a threat in an inciting narrative (to terrorism) is specific, likely and imminent. That in itself has placed a threshold so high that few prosecutors will indict an inciter, and even if there is an indictment the likelihood of a conviction is not high. Focusing on a direct link between incitement and violence has put the fight against incitement in a practical strait jacket.

Given that reactive police measures against incitement are very sparingly used and given that proactive measures have a long way to go to demonstrate

---

5 Part 1 crimes are serious crimes against the person and against property reported to the FBI: *Criminal homicide, Forcible rape, Robbery, Aggravated assault Burglary (breaking or entering), Larceny-theft (except motor vehicle theft), Motor vehicle theft, and Arson.* Part 2 crimes for which data is collected include: Other assaults (simple), Forgery and counterfeiting, Fraud, Embezzlement, Stolen property; buying, receiving, possessing, Vandalism, Weapons; carrying, possessing, etc., Prostitution and commercialized vice, Sex offenses (except forcible rape, prostitution, and commercialized vice), Drug abuse violations, Gambling, Offenses against the family and children, Driving under the influence, Liquor laws, Drunkenness, Disorderly conduct, Vagrancy, All other offense, Suspicion, Curfew and loitering laws (persons under age 18), and Runaways (persons under age 18).

6 Greene, Jack R. and Stephen D. Mastrofski (Eds.) COMMUNITY POLICING: RHETORIC OR REALITY (1988).

effectiveness, the question is then raised as to the overall role of police in addressing incitement and perhaps the overarching question is how to develop an effective strategy to deal with incitement.

Also, given that the West, in general, refrains from infringing on free speech, this fundamentally gives inciters an almost free hand to say almost whatever they want. The cases of virulent incitement in Australia, Canada, Israel, the UK, and the US prove that it can be done with virtual immunity. Moreover, incitement is no longer limited to "local production." If ten years ago there may have been around a couple dozen radical web sites, today there are more than 10,000. It is the export of inspiring hate and hate-inspiring narratives that urges individuals to commit terrorism and violent acts. We are shocked when it happens in a Western country and more shocked as it gets closer to home, but terrorism is the "currency" of worldwide, daily practice with numerous casualties.[7]

Incitement is a much wider concept than a clear text that directly leads to violence and it has a wide spectrum of elements such as hate, vilification, dehumanization, incitement to violence and then violence itself. With the limited impact of the legal approach on incitement, it is important to explore additional modalities of addressing incitement. Even if legal measures against incitement may prove effective, those measures are relatively few and usually are taken after violence has already occurred. Such measures could be taken mostly against "locals," as it is highly unlikely that the propagandists who write in on-line magazines, such as *Inspire* and *Dabiq,* will be brought to justice in a western country.

In the same manner, it is not a likely measure against incitement by clerics in mosques, newspaper columnists, commentators, political figures and the like who incessantly produce the entire gamut of vitriolic incitement and "export" it from "remote" sites for "local use." Short of very few military attacks (by drones) there is very little legal or other counter-effort against the inciting messages.

In order for the legal system to more effectively address incitement, it is suggested to adopt an overall comprehensive strategic approach that will make it a national and international priority to counter incitement in its various forms. This means that to cope with the challenges that incitement poses, it is imperative to move from a legal-centered and police-centered approach to a comprehensive proactive approach that is multi-pronged. Namely, this approach should identify the sources of incitement, the messages, content, context, use,

7 *See:* the Global Terrorism Database at https://www.start.umd.edu/gtd/ with more than 150,000 documented attacks.

source, end-recipients, frequency, purpose, author(s), facilitators, supporters and potential sources to counter the incitement.

This means that incitement needs to be identified at an early stage and proper intervention should be designed to mitigate and counter it prior to radicalization and violent acts. A community-based approach, the building of partnerships, coordination of activities, and the structuring of proper narratives and counter narratives are crucial steps. Not immediately defining incitement as a criminal act allows community groups to focus on such activity and counter it without having to worry about probable cause and legal proceedings. It does not mean that due process is ignored. On the contrary, it will be called on at a later stage when it is possible to link the incitement to terrorism. Until then, civil society can contribute a major part in the effort to cope with incitement and its aftermath.

Here is an outline for a suggested comprehensive incitement-centered approach to countering incitement:

- Identify and define what is incitement
- Early identification of incitement
- Diagnose its sources
- Identify support of and receptivity to incitement
- Identify potential sources that can be used to counter inciting narrative/content
- Identify effective methods of countering incitement
- Offer a multi-prong proactive approach based on:
    - legal formulation
        - legislative effort
        - enforcement
    - public policy
    - social policy
    - policing strategies – specifically, community policing
    - media and educational methods
    - coordination of activities
    - commitment and perseverance
    - developing, maintaining and enhancing community partnerships
    - delivery of services to counter the potential impact of incitement

Index

Printed in the United States
By Bookmasters